GEO/GRAPHICS

Simple Form Graphics in Print and Motion

Edited & published
by
viction:ary

Geo/Graphics

Simple Form Graphics
in Print and Motion

First published and distributed by
viction:workshop ltd.

viction:ary™

viction:workshop ltd.
Unit C, 7/F, Seabright Plaza, 9-23 Shell Street,
North Point, Hong Kong
Url: www.victionary.com   Email: we@victionary.com
www.facebook.com/victionworkshop
www.twitter.com/victionary_
www.weibo.com/victionary

Edited and produced by viction:workshop ltd.

Concepts & art direction by Victor Cheung
Book design by viction:workshop ltd.

ISBN 978-988-19439-2-7

Printed and bound in China

Our world is patched up in shapes. In architecture, typefaces or infographics, squares, triangles and circles provide the basic frames and forms. Because of their modularity, almost everything can be constructed from or reduced into shapes. Together with colours, they function as the universal token of meanings, representing abstract concepts and physical objects in religion, communication and graphic art.

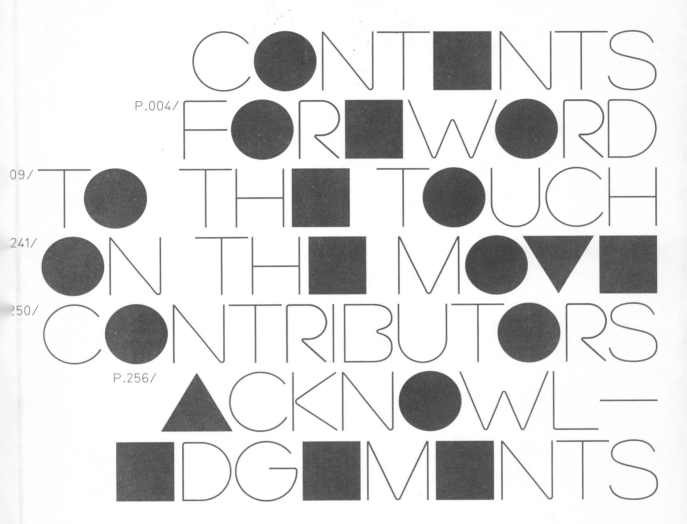

CONT■NTS

P.004/ FOR■WORD

09/ TO TH■ TOUCH

241/ ON TH■ MOV■

250/ CONTRIBUT■RS

P.256/ ▲CKNOWL—■DG■M■NTS

FORWORD

As graphic designers we use geometric shapes in two different ways — visible geometry and invisible geometry.

Visible geometry utilises shapes, elements and patterns to form the visual component of the design work or, indeed, to act as individual complementary and competing elements within that art. Basically, it can be anything of geometric form that is intended as a visible element in the design.

Invisible geometry on the other hand is just that, it can't be seen but it is the glue that binds the design elements together. It is the negative space creating tension or balance. It is the grid linking elements together. It connects and disconnects and creates movement and voice. Designers use the invisible to make the visible tangible and dynamic, which is the true mark of design that both challenges and communicates.

Geometry and its ubiquitous circle, square and triangle are indeed the most basic of design tools and do not belong to a particular style or artistic period. In recent times however, there has been a substantial rise in their use. This increase in appreciation of the power of geometric forms in contemporary graphic design can perhaps be attributed to a reconnection with the influence of early 20th century art and design movements such as Bauhaus or Modernism. Geometric shapes are not a new invention, but designers are continuously discovering, innovating and interpreting them and continuously applying newer and fresher treatments to match today's currency.

Whether you utilise a circle, pattern or an underlying grid system, you are employing the use of geometric shapes to form structure and connection within the design. Once understood and respected, these elements can provide you with a powerful and limitless array of design tools. Enjoy them.

Motherbird

We live in a world with an overdose of visual stimuli — ads everywhere, contacts on Facebook posting pictures every five minutes, YouTube viral videos... tonnes of visual data are thrown at us everyday and we can't digest them. As a designer I find this reality as the initial problem to solve— this is my catalyst. When you look at things through the glass of simplicity you start to realise how human loves to overcomplicate their lives, and it's exciting to think how everything could be done in a whole different way.

As a graphic designer I have worked in a strange mix of different projects: I've created icons for banks, posters for recording studios, logos for telecommunication companies and packaging for alcohol brands. I've also been involved in innovation and product design, interactive and web apps for Europe and Asia. In all of these projects I kept my conviction of how things have to be done, following my simplistic approach to what a good design should be. I humbly conceive my job as merely a way to do things more accessible, more organised, more harmonic and why not, more beautiful. It's also a process of communication, where shapes, colours and typography collide to express a message to an audience.

I've learned that sometimes what really affects the visual result of a design is the part that cannot be seen: grids and negative space. If you compare a particular design with the human anatomy, the grids will be like the spine and bones that hold the whole body. They determine the exact position where the parts will be and how the body will look like. The negative space – or the empty space in the composition – can focus the viewer's attention to the visual elements and make them more prominent. This is to me the key of simplicity in design, having the ability to say something with nothing. Geometry also plays an important role, as it's the most boiled down essence of any form. Using pure shapes in a design helps to keep the level of abstraction and to create straightforward and eye-catchy results. Some designers tend to use sophisticated shapes and effects in order to create something striking and nice – sometimes this might be counterproductive and it might make the design less efficient by overcomplicating the message.

Minimalist design is trending up today, as it was in the 60s and early 70s – we're coming back to the simple. The movement could be perfectly defined by the words of French writer Antoine de Saint-Exupéry, who defined the style as being 'not when there's nothing more to add, but when there's nothing left to take away'. Some important brands also are following this trend and they are simplifying their logos by taking away all the elements that are not essential or by focusing on their representative colour. It's also a matter of contrast, in a world where everyone wants his or her voice to be heard, a whisper can be louder than a shout. Simple graphics can be more striking than sophisticated ones. Simplicity allows people to complete the shapes with their own knowledge and experiences, allowing some interpretation and creating more meaningful pieces of work. I like to think that 'Simple is the new clever' in a way that you can say more with less.

Genís Carreras
— Simple is the new clever

"A design should have some tension and some expression in itself. I like to compare it with the lines on a football field. It is a strict grid. In this grid you play a game and these can be nice games or very boring games." — Wim Crouwel

This book aims to capture the work by current practitioners of design who employ the use of bold, simple geometry. The use of these graphic forms is certainly nothing new. It is a visual language that has remained surprisingly similar in appearance to the time it was introduced.

Great pioneers of this graphic medium laid the foundations for much of the work you will see in these pages, accomplishing extraordinarily innovative, powerful and bold works. I think it is worth mentioning a few of my own personal heros in this field to whom I am indebted.

Swiss-born Karl Gerstner (b. 1930) was not only a hugely influential graphic designer but also an artist who devoted his later life to colour. His groundbreaking use of grids as well as his systematic approach to design helped to form a graphic language that still resonates today. American-born Sol LeWitt (1928 – 2007) worked as a graphic designer in his youth and later became a hugely influential artist associated with the conceptual and minimalist art movements. I find all his work fascinating, but have a particular obsession with his bold and systematic wall drawings. Josef Müller-Brockmann (1914 – 1996) was regarded as the leading practitioner and theorist of the Swiss style of graphic design. His work sought a direct approach to communicating information, often employing minimal geometric forms.

These artists helped to form a universal visual language that not only still exists today, but a language that is completely ingrained within our current understanding of what design is and should be. Sometimes I arrive at a solution in my own work after a long period of experimentation that I believe has some originality. Only to find a few weeks later something incredibly similar lying in the pages of an old dusty design book by a graphics master of the past that I have yet to encounter. Instead of finding this experience disheartening and frustrating I have learnt to be encouraged and inspired by it. By rediscovering the paths and processes that these designers took, I am able to develop and build upon their ideas and methods to create my own.

Employing geometry in my work allows me to create structured methods and creative processes. But it also offers a limitless plane of possibilities, that grants me a great deal of freedom and pleasure when making images. I sometimes think my creative process is akin to the act of making music. Balance, harmony and repetition are key factors I consider when using geometric forms to create my work. It's often intuitive and hard to teach. Simple geometry provides me with a mode of expression that I feel I'll be exploring for many years to come. The more I learn and discover the more I realise just how little I know. My work is not only a celebration of shape, form and colour but also a celebration of life in a wider sense. Geometry allows me to explore my interest in the converging pathways of art, music and science as its mathematical nature applies to them all.

Experimenting with and simplifying abstract geometric forms seems to me a logical way in which we as designers attempt to understand and communicate the chaotic world around us. This book contains a snapshot of applied geometry of the here and now, but I feel work of this nature will continue to intrigue and challenge designers far into the future, as it has done well into the past.

Jack Featherstone

TO
THE
TOUCH

Every designer sees a different quality in shapes. Some relate them to childhood games. Others reckon them simply as forms — with balanced mathematical structure to work as planes or grids, strokes or dots.

Shapes are what we used to construct memories. And today, they are the strategy to attain efficiency, contrast the nature and pattern the world. This section presents the infinity of shapes in 131 promotional art, textile prints, brand identity, environmental graphics, crafts, photo-log and life-size installations you can touch and hug!

Hey Christmas 2011

Studio work for Christmas celebration. Ten tinted limpid triangle plates were config-
ured into a simple yet blissful pinwheel star and photographed to
produce prints and digital wallpaper for studio clients and friends.

Design: Hey

Hey

heystudio.es

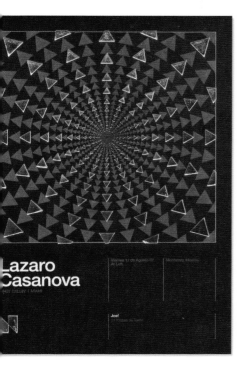

Lazaro
Casanova

[illegible] GALLERY | MIAMI

Viernes 17 de Agosto 07   Monterrey, México.
At Loft

Joe!

MSTRKRFT
MODULAR | CANADA

Jueves 22 de Noviembre   Monterrey, México.
Pabellón Tec

Hell-o.
Mi Jason de oro.

Nrmal

Nrmal celebrates music and art and organises the Festival Nrmal once a year.
These premium Swiss-grid-based flyers were part of their branding system designed for
concerts in Monterrey, Mexico. The geometry of Helvetica Neue and basic op-art
illustrations delivered the ambiance at its best.

Design: Face. / Client: Nrmal

Pier Bucci
CHILE | CROSSTOWN REBELS

29 / 03 / 2007   Monterrey, México.
At Loft

Bienvenido.
Identifíque lo Nrmal quien pueda, adhiérase quien quiera.

Mental
IMECA | MÉXICO
Quiero Club
DJ SET | HAPPY FI

03 / 05 / 2007   Monterrey, México.
At Loft

Ahoi.
El motivo es el baile.

Noguera & Vintró

Identity for gift and stationery distributor, Noguera & Vintró, is led by its initials abstracted from the alphabets' shared structures. A grey paper similar to the candid unprocessed paperboard was used for a honest brand image, accented by a sharp orange tone.

Design: Marnich Associates / Client: Noguera & Vintró

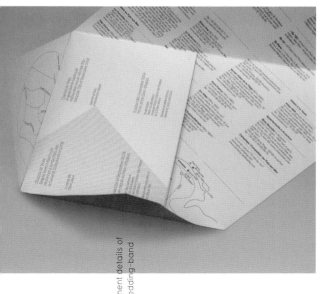

Artworklove Wedding Invitation

A self-enveloping wedding invitation, comprised of all maps, pertinent details of the wedding and RSVP cards for the attendees. The motif of a wedding-band was reduced to a circle, dipped in Pantone gold.

Design: Artworklove

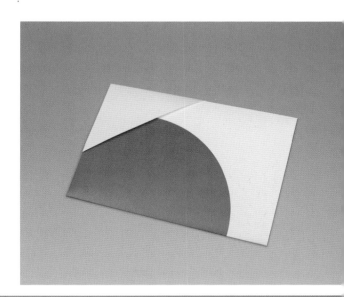

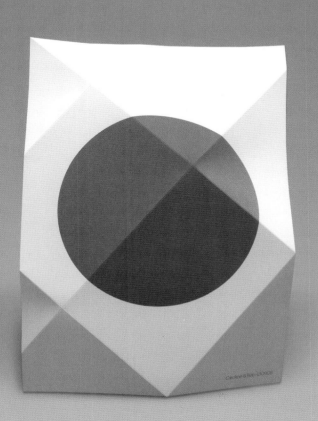

013

Calendar 2012

In-house calendar cards with each month denoted by the ascending facets of different polygons devised by Gerard Miró. While January is a flat, plain square, December is multidimensional hexagon with 12 faces perceptible from the front.

Design: Lo Siento

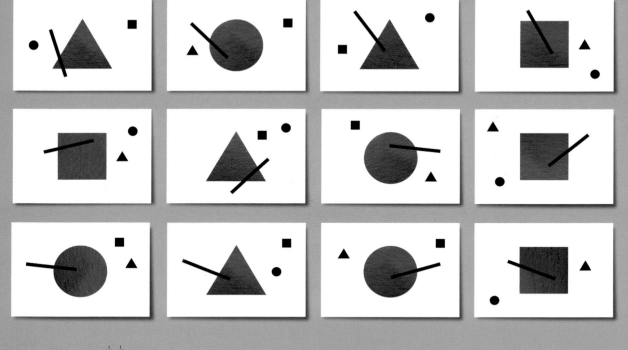

Fundación General CSIC Cards

Dynamism and diversity are the key. With an array of primitive shapes dancing around a glossy blue figure at the core, the card introduces the foundation's interactive role in channelling knowledge and skills to the world of research.

Design: Loop-Loop Studio / Client: Fundación General CSIC

Science and Innovation in Spain

Metaphorically, innovations are like puzzles composed of simple factors. For FECYT's *Analysis on Science and Innovation in Spain* report, a different symmetric shape was assigned to denote a change of chapter in the study concerning the development of science and innovation in Spain.

Design: Loop-Loop Studio / Client: Foundation for Science and Technology (FECYT)

HQ:D&B Flyer

Flyer outlining HD club's drum and bass nights for the first half of 2010. Along with a clean and structured type, the central graphics convey strong beats to the eye in two colours on a 100% recycled pulp board contrasting the gloss.

Design: Ross Gunter / Client: HQ:D&B

Flyer content

HQ Drum & Bass
Oxford's Longest
Running D&B Night

The Cellar Bar, Off Frewin Court
Cornmarket Street, Oxford

February—May 2010 Events

Marcus Intalex* (Soul:R)
Stumasta (DSM) Freehand
Pez (Break₍thru₎)   *Marcus Intalex 90 Minute Set

Loxy (Metalheadz // Cylon)
& Jubei (Metalheadz)
Azonica // Freehand
Script MC & Combat Collins

Stylecraft Adelaide Showroom Opening Invitation

To beat the drum for Stylecraft's new furniture showroom, THERE livened up the invite with the brand's colour, symbol and a bit of throb. The thrill was yielded in two ways, with both silver and clear foils on duplexed fluro pink or black stock.

Design: THERE / Client: Stylecraft

GLUE Identity

GLUE specialises in working with youths who are struggling to sustain education. As to highlight its devotion to forging links and creating bonds in the community, each stationery item feature two contrasting patterns to be united with the name 'GLUE'.

Design: Magpie Studio / Client: GLUE

**GENEVIEVE MAITLAND HUDSON
DIRECTOR**

+44 (0)7950 485 509 GENEVIEVE@GLUE-WEB.COM

29 LOVE WALK, LONDON, SE5 8AD
+44 (0)20 7450 3508 WWW.GLUE-WEB.COM

FORGING LINKS, BUILDING BRIDGES, CREATING BONDS

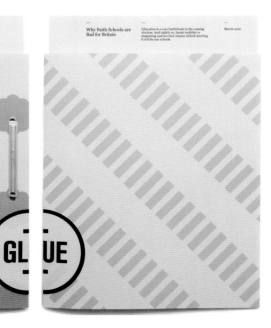

Why Faith Schools are
Bad for Britain

Education is a core battlefront in the coming
election. And rightly so. Social mobility is
stagnating and our best chance of kick-starting
it will be our schools.

March 2010

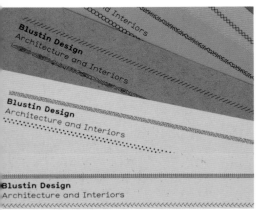

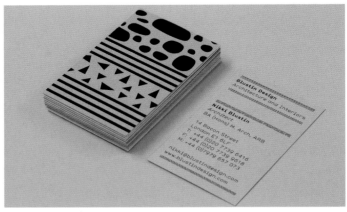

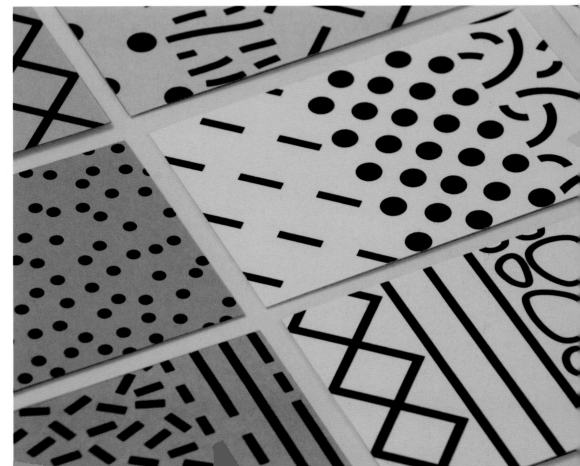

Blustin Design Stationery

Architects use hatch patterns to designate building materials on drawings, so Mind borrowed these lines and dots to define this British architectural practice on its business cards. A humble range of colour stock were taken to elevate the marks.

Design: Mind Design / Client: Blustin Design

023

Resort Wall-Calendar 2012

Strangely enough, Resort Studio's calendar can be reckoned as a perpetual one for its absence of days. Devised in coincide with the studio's inception, the wall calendar asks its users to flip a page and understand the studio's graphic approach through a different illustration each month.

Design: Resort Studio

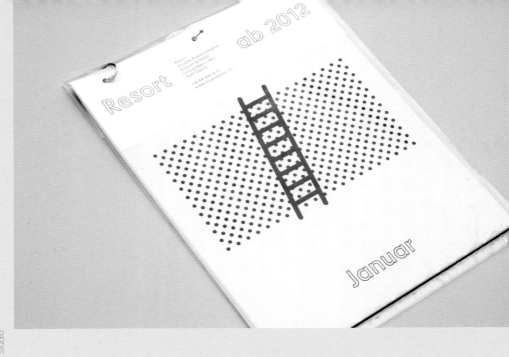

Februar

November

Juni

Juli

Mai

Nachtschicht #5

Flyer for an open night event, *Nachtschicht* (nightshift), at the St.Gallen Museum of the Arts. The graphics narrated the course of sunset and sky colour variations from day to night. Text grids at the back echoed the sun's shift on the front.

Design: Larissa Kasper and Rosario Florio / Client: Kunstverein St.Gallen

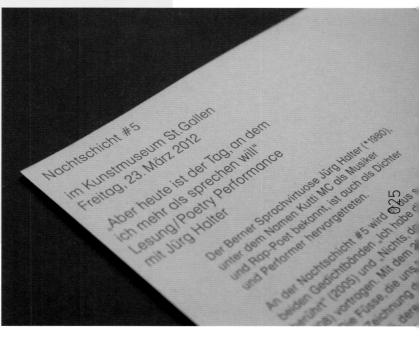

Nachtschicht #5

im Kunstmuseum St.Gallen
Freitag, 23. März 2012

„Aber heute ist der Tag, an dem
ich mehr als sprechen will"
Lesung/Poetry Performance
mit Jürg Halter

Der Berner Sprachvirtuose Jürg Halter (*1980),
unter dem Namen Kutti MC als Musiker
und Rap-Poet bekannt, ist auch als Dichter
und Performer hervorgetreten.

An der Nachtschicht #5 wird

025

Basic Shapes Cups

MusaWorkLab™'s double wall fine faience cups bear the studio's name in an artistically-designed artwork originally composed by Jorge Trindade and João Seco in 2005. The prints were reproduced as limited edition cups for sale.

Design: MusaWorkLab™

Shelf Lamp

The small lamps measuring 20cm high with a pine base and round lacquered shade are manufactured to light up shelves. With the bulb installed behind the opaque disc, light diffuses along the edge and emits an aura of mystery on the rack.

Design: Andreas Engesvik / Manufacture & client: David Design

WWW

The 'shelf' archetype is designed anew with functional surfaces dissolved into spaced out strings. The converted forms and functions of a shelf is customised to explore the abolished limits of space and time, especially of materials in a digitalised society.

Design: Viktor Matic

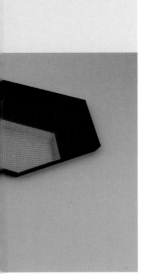

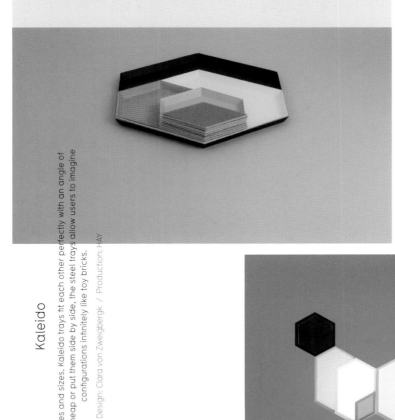

Kaleido

Coming in five shapes and sizes, Kaleido trays fit each other perfectly with an angle of 120 degree. Make a heap or put them side by side, the steel trays allow users to imagine configurations infinitely like toy bricks.

Design: Clara von Zweigbergk / Production: HAY

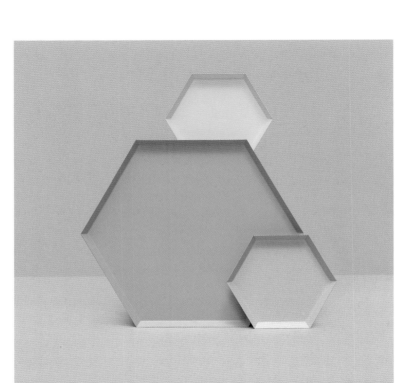

COASTAL

Coastal & South City

Korbel-Bowers' posters reflect his fondness for things going on around San Francisco. *Coastal* (top) depicts the colour interactions between the city's urban and natural landscape in the coastal neighbourhood. *South City* (bottom) is a playful recall of the city's airport he saw everyday as a kid from his home on a hillside.

Design: Matthew Korbel-Bowers

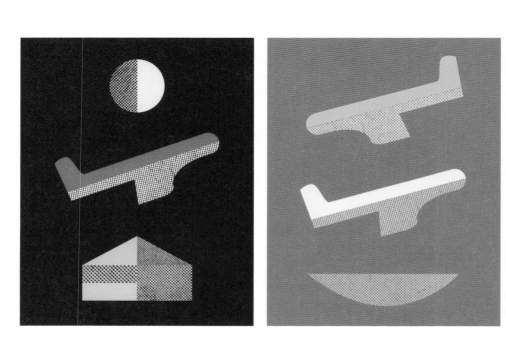

Kiblind Magazine Cover

With an aim to condense all topics on handicrafts, architecture and graphic of *Kiblind*'s 2010 winter issue in one frame, Château Vacant created a rough puzzle with found wood blocks for photography that were partly painted and partly ripped. *Kiblind* is a free cultural periodical distributed in Lyon, France.

Design: Château-vacant / Client: Kiblind Magazine

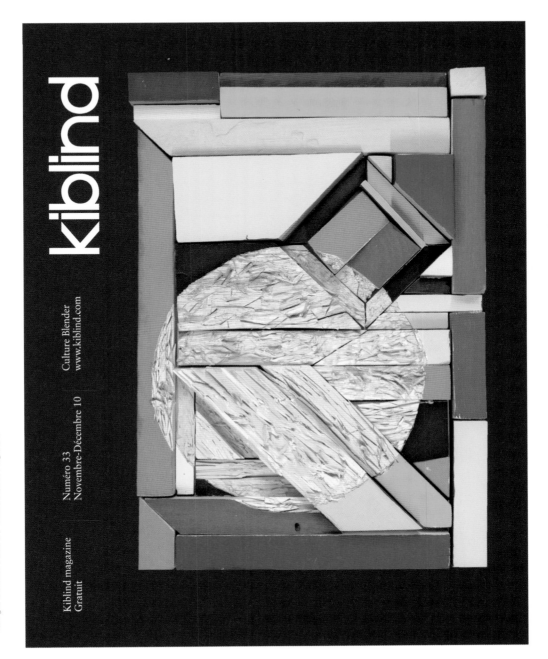

kiblind

Kiblind magazine
Gratuit

Numéro 33
Novembre-Décembre 10

Culture Blender
www.kiblind.com

032

Your Type of Printer

Your Type of Printer is conceived as an arrangement of large solid colours to show off Digital-press' solid colour printing. Adopting the Bauhaus aesthetics, the custom type created from primary shapes and colours offers a second meaning for "type" in the catchphrase.

Design: Mark Gowing Design / Client: Digitalpress

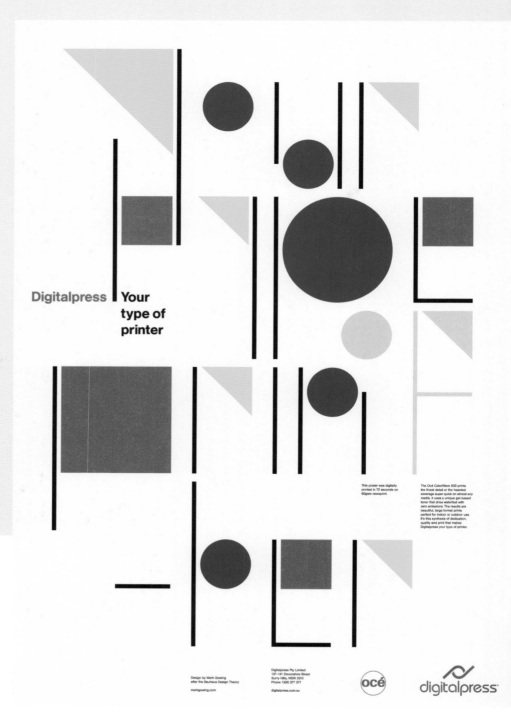

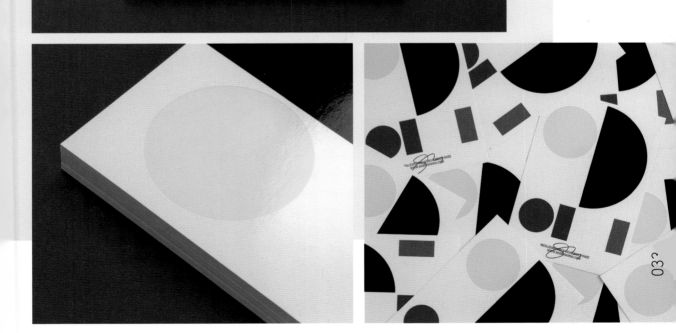

seb navarro design 2011

With modernist spirits at the heart, Navarro developed a descontructed figure "2011" to greet the new year. Like dreams, the composition was abstract and mysterious, aiming to release everyone's imagination by design.

Design: seb navarro design

K11 Design Store X'mas 2011

Featuring a conceptual Christmas tree as the centrepiece, the festive gift wrappers, tags and leaflets were commissioned to promote Christmas shopping at K11 Design Store. All designer items available from the store were reduced to decorate the tree, fueling the air with more festive imaginations and joy.

Design: BLOW / Client: K11 Design Store

035

Børk Gift Wrapping Paper

Børk Gift Wrappers are made to work also as posters alone. Contrary to the traditional seamless recurring patterns, the Scandinavian-style illustrations on the paper spread out on two themes – birds and fish species rendered in triangles and circles, and altitude lines of glaciers with various weather symbols.

Design: Thorleifur Gunnar Gíslason

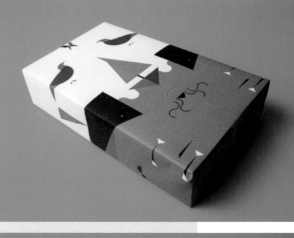

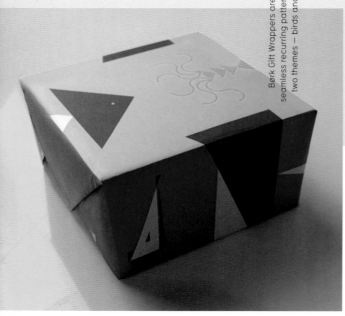

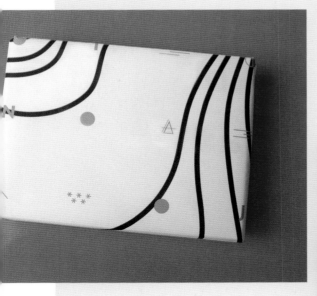

037

Hello Studio Constantine

Studio Constantine's approach to their own brand is defined by the meeting of concept and craft. Geometry, colour, typography and format are used in preference to the norm of type or icon lock-up. Each item serves individually and together to identify the studio's belief and pragmatism in minimal colours.

Design: Studio Constantine / Photo: Andrew Schweitzer /
Conceptual building blocks: TreeHorn Design

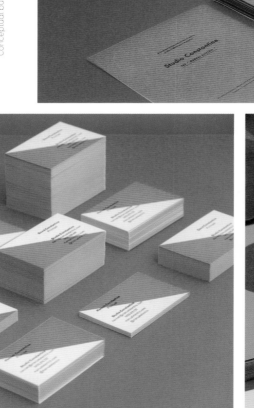

Enterprise and Labour

Streaming at a regular beat, these covers envision a continuous flow of analytical statistics and information from the Ministry of Enterprise and Labour of Catalonia. Each pattern is allocated to a different topic that concerns both employers and employees.

Design: Hey / Client: Government of Catalonia / Photo: Roc Canals

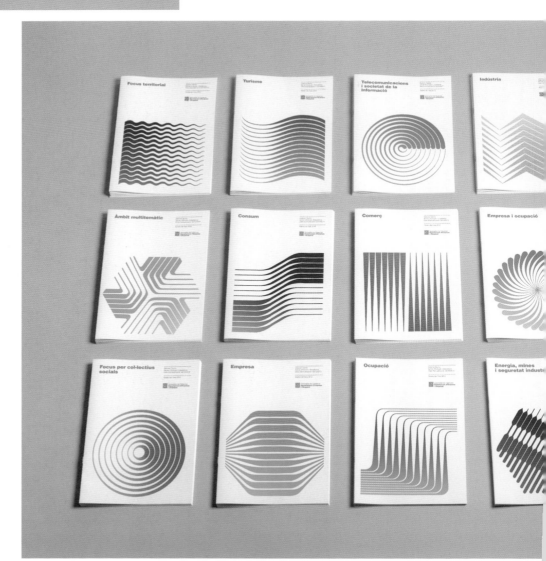

Projecta't

Projecta't is a program organised by the Catalan government to provide network and support for entrepreneurs' consolidation plans and growth. The poster stressed growth and expansion with layers and progressively warm colours to outline the project's aim and role.

Design: Hey / Client: Government of Catalonia

TALES
OF
WHERE
WE
ARE
GOING

我们的皮草之旅

Kopenhagen Fur China Expo

A bilingual publication for Kopenhagen Fur's appearance in EXPO 2010 Shanghai China.
The covers expanded on the auction house's visual identity, emphasising mink fur as the ultimate
luxury material for fashion, with a corner snipped off for a sneak preview.

Design: Re-public / Client: Kopenhagen Fur

KOPENHAGEN
FUR

10th Anniversary Party Invitation

Invitation design for public relations agency, Weber Shandwick's 10th anniversary party at the Saatchi Gallery. Graphic elements were kept to a minimal with only black and white foil on boards posted in matching envelopes.

Design: Ross Gunter / Client: Weber Shandwick

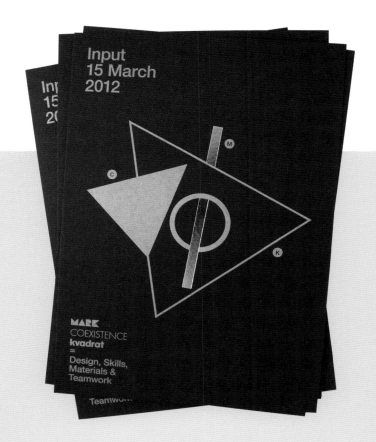

MARK
COEXISTENCE
kvadrat
=
Design, Skills,
Materials &
Teamwork

Teamwork

MARK

MARK's furniture and lifestyle products are environmentally, economically and socially sustainable. Championing design as well as craftsmanship, MARK conceived a wood modular logomark to convey its ethos across the brand. For its yearly catalogue, emphasis was placed on its palette to indicate evolution on its product range.

Design: A-Side Studio / Client: MARK

Blau Menus

Named "Blau", the restaurant draws its inspirations from the sea of Costa Brava that characterises the town of Begur where the kitchen locates. Three patterns evocative of undulating water surfaces were composed for Blau's lunch, dinner and drink menus, to restate the theme and its minimalistic approach to food.

Design: Mucho / Client: Restaurante Blau

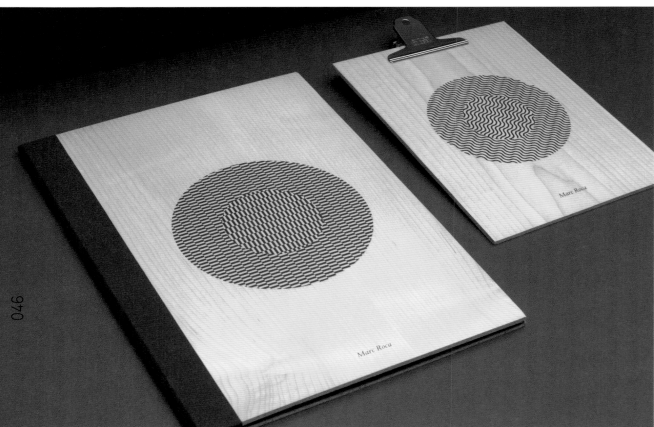

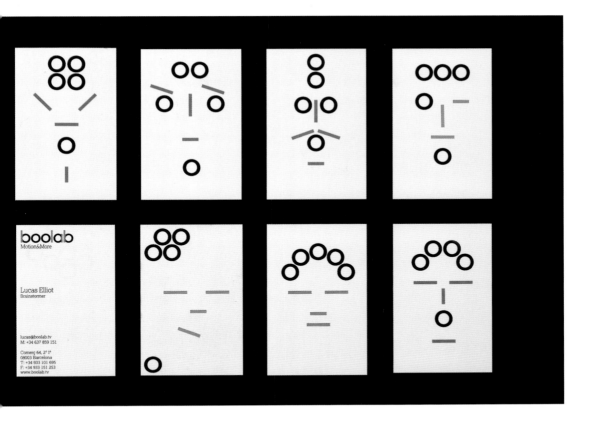

boolab Motion&More

Boolab is a bubbly production house based in Barcelona. Seeing a chance to deconstruct the name into five circles and four strokes, Mucho visualised Boolab's personality and dynamism with a brilliant spectrum of things from the elements and a hint in the logotype. A short animation was also produced to picture the graphic game.

Design: Mucho / Client: boolab Motion&More

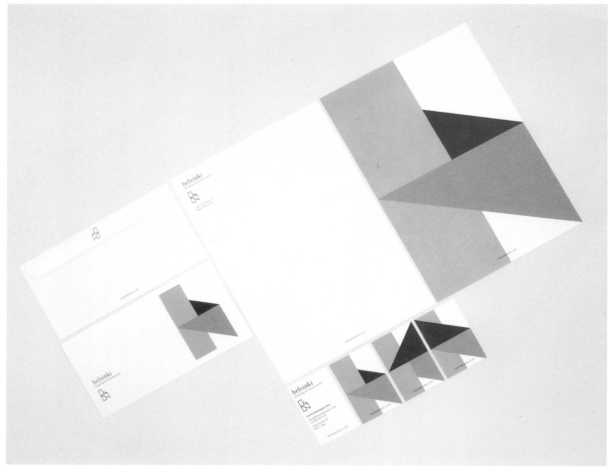

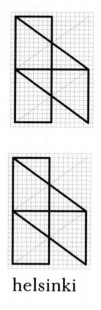

helsinki

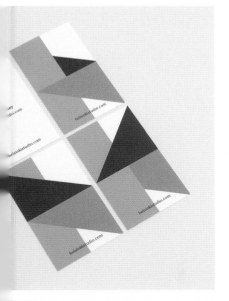

Helsinki Studio

Greatly influenced by Finnish culture, Helsinki promises to bring branding strategies and communications alive with tailored solutions at their Barcelona base. The variable visual code was a rhythmic and dynamic take on such vision of the brand.

Design: Francesc Moret Vayreda, Andrés Requena / Client: Helsinki studio

Jultid

Ten pieces of handpainted birch blocks were manufactured and sent around for free renditions of Christmas scenes during the seasonal holidays. Jultid is Swedish for "Christmas Time" and the blocks were meant to shine on bookshelves as a simple "3D Christmas card".

Design: Maija Fredrika

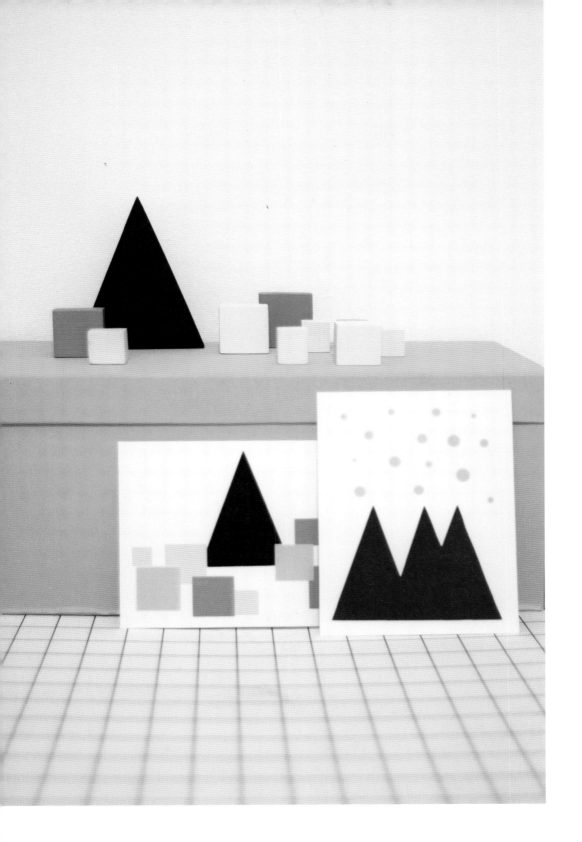

Designinstituttet

These brochure and display shelf were developed in hands with G*R*I*G for Design Institute's counter at a trade fair. Using black MDF boards as the skeleton of the shelf, Heydays devised an assemblage of geometric modules that can graphically describe the school's programmes and materialise as the units of a rack at once.

Design: Heydays, G*R*I*G architects / Client: Designinstituttet

Der du lærer grunnleggende design

Designinstituttet er en ettårig
fagskole i Oslo som tilbyr grunnleggende innføring i designfag.

NTU Art & Design Degree Show Invites '09

Invitations for the *Nottingham Trent University Art and Design Degree Show 2009*. Typeface featuring letters customised with stripes, dots and net patterns introduced the theme in black foil on the front with details in silver on the back.

Design: Andrew Townsend (Un.titled) / Client: Nottingham Trent University

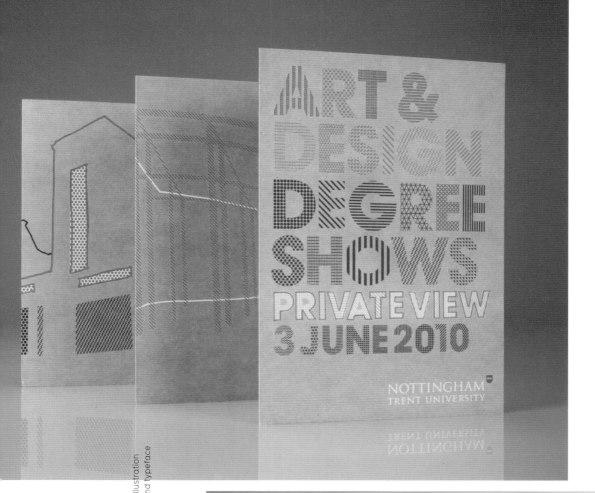

NTU Art & Design Degree Show Invite '10

Invitation for the *Nottingham Trent University Art and Design Degree Show 2010*. The illustration outlined the main buildings where the show took place, with patterned lines, shades and typeface cohering 2009's theme in violet and pink.

Design: Andrew Townsend (Un.titled) / Client: Nottingham Trent University

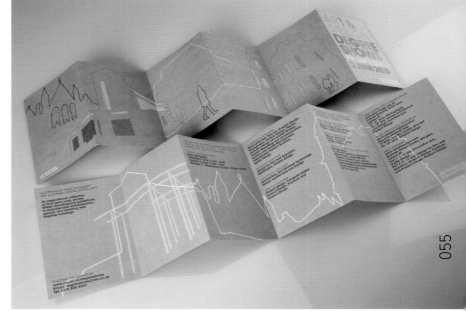

Nuna & Brand Book

A revolutionary sensation of ice lolly comes in Nuna, which claims "Form Follows Taste", developed by Neubau in hands with artist-and-architect Manu Kumar. Neubau was responsible for the overall product design, branding and identity design.

Design: Neubau (NeubauBerlin.Com) / Client: Nuna World GmbH

●Muna Popsicle   D: Gandl/Kruez, Neubau (Berlin) 2006; exclusively developed for Muna World Gmbh.

The product design of Muna is registered nationally and internationally as an independent 3-D brand.
2006©2011 (c) Copyright by Muna World Gmbh. All rights reserved.

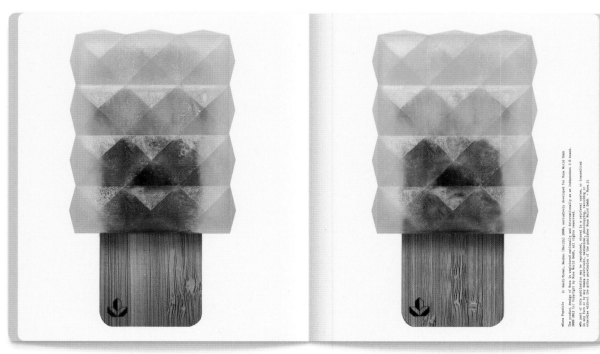

●Muna Popsicle   D: Gandl/Kruez, Neubau (Berlin) 2006; exclusively developed for Muna World Gmbh.

The product design of Muna is registered nationally and internationally as an independent 3-D brand.
2006©2011 (c) Copyright by Muna World Gmbh. All rights reserved.

Bexel

These packaging designs were part of the rebranding scheme for Mexican construction supplies company, Bexel. Besides its content, functions and uses, the new solution also lays stress on the efficiency and aesthetic one can effortlessly attain with Bexel's products, such as mortar and grout.

Design: Face. / Client: Bexel

Brüken Tile Adhesives Packaging

Aesthetically pleasing without much extravagant details, these tile adhesive packages are meant to be a discreet reminder of the creative aspects of construction work. On a simple white background, being the adhesive base of the product, the diamond shapes resembled the iconic tile designs.

Design: mousegraphics / Client: Petrocoll S.A.

BRÜKEN 0-8mm

BRÜKEN 0-8mm

BRÜKEN 0-8mm

BRÜKEN SUPER

BRÜKEN FLEX

BRÜKEN EXTRA

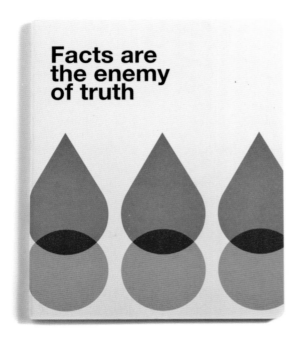

Facts are
the enemy
of truth

Life is far
too important
to be taken
seriously

A writer
should
write
with his
eyes and
a painter
paint
with his
ears

Doubt grows with
knowledge.

Ogami Collection

Logo and graphic design for a new brand and its notebook range compiled of materials manufactured using stone instead of traditional paper. Inspirations for the graphics was the clean International Typographic Style with quotations, turning them into exceptional stationery with a contemporary taste and unique personality.

Design: Officemilano / Client: Cartorama Group,
Paolo Frello & Partners

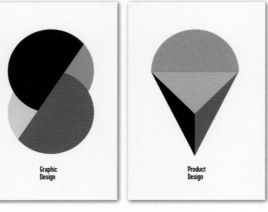

Interior
Design

Graphic
Design

Product
Design

Fashion
Design

ADS international design & art center

Pasted at ADS design school's office, the four posters underline the spirit and values
the school advocates towards design. The compound elements also serve as a conceptual depiction of the four design programs operated at the school.

Design: Studio Tada / Client: ADS international design & art center

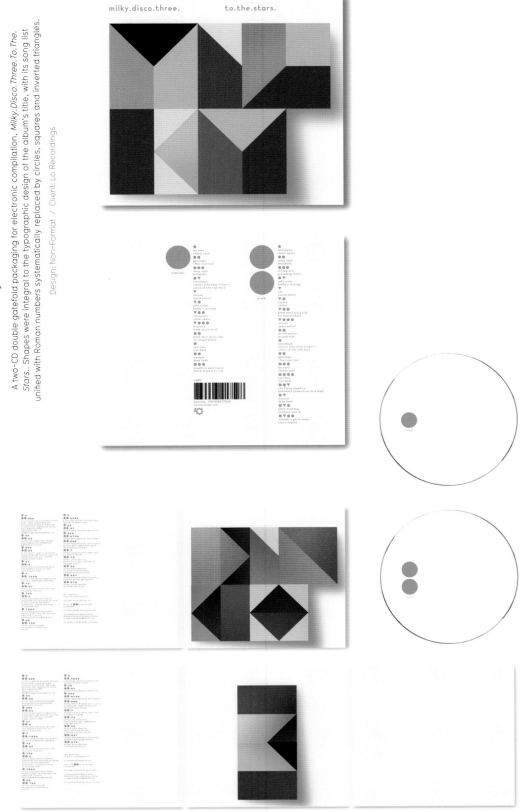

Milky Disco Three – To The Stars

A two-CD double gatefold packaging for electronic compilation, *Milky.Disco.Three.To.The. Stars.*. Shapes were integral to the typographic design of the album's title, with its song list unified with Roman numbers systematically replaced by circles, squares and inverted triangles.

Design: Non-Format / Client: Lo Recordings

DE-SIGN FOR KIDS

El diseño juega un papel fundamental en nuestra sociedad dado que actualmente impregna casi todas las cosas que rodean nuestra vida cotidiana. Es importante enseñar a los niños, que actualmente y por inercia asumen el diseño con total naturalidad, que éste, en realidad, es fruto de un proceso intelectual previo muchas veces largo y dificultoso. Para que aprendan a valorarlo y diferenciarlo, **Design for Kids**, acercará el diseño a los niños, a través de la realización de talleres y minicursos adaptados a cada edad en colegios.

www.mrmarcelschool.com

DE-SIGN FOR KIDS

El diseño juega un papel fundamental en nuestra sociedad dado que actualmente impregna casi todas las cosas que rodean nuestra vida cotidiana. Es importante enseñar a los niños, que actualmente y por inercia asumen el diseño con total naturalidad, que éste, en realidad, es fruto de un proceso intelectual previo muchas veces largo y dificultoso. Para que aprendan a valorarlo y diferenciarlo, **Design for Kids**, acercará el diseño a los niños, a través de la realización de talleres y minicursos adaptados a cada edad en colegios.

www.mrmarcelschool.com

DE-SIGN FOR KIDS

El diseño juega un papel fundamental en nuestra sociedad dado que actualmente impregna casi todas las cosas que rodean nuestra vida cotidiana. Es importante enseñar a los niños, que actualmente y por inercia asumen el diseño con total naturalidad, que éste, en realidad, es fruto de un proceso intelectual previo muchas veces largo y dificultoso. Para que aprendan a valorarlo y diferenciarlo, **Design for Kids**, acercará el diseño a los niños, a través de la realización de talleres y minicursos adaptados a cada edad en colegios.

www.mrmarcelschool.com

DE-SIGN FOR KIDS

El diseño juega un papel fundamental en nuestra sociedad dado que actualmente impregna casi todas las cosas que rodean nuestra vida cotidiana. Es importante enseñar a los niños, que actualmente y por inercia asumen el diseño con total naturalidad, que éste, en realidad, es fruto de un proceso intelectual previo muchas veces largo y dificultoso. Para que aprendan a valorarlo y diferenciarlo, **Design for Kids**, acercará el diseño a los niños, a través de la realización de talleres y minicursos adaptados a cada edad en colegios.

www.mrmarcelschool.com

DESIGN FOR KIDS

Design for Kids is a workshop set to bring the art of design to kids. On the front, the graphics pointed to the joy of creation with colourful animals derived from tans. Individual units reappeared on the reverse, setting off details of the concept and turning each poster as part of a bigger puzzle piece.

Design: Sants / Serif / Client: Mr. Marcel School

I have always struggled with making decisions and what I like on the one day I might question on the next. People often see the variation in our work as playful but in all honesty this is often just indecisiveness. As longer I am working as a designer as more confused I am. Although I am not sure if this is a good or a bad thing. You are asking me for my favourite shape? I like squares because they are organised, but I also like circles which are more holistic. If I have to decide I would pick the Hexagon. It is somewhere in between but without being a compromise. Quite the opposite, the hexagon works best as a building block for pattern and all kind of structures.

Mind Design

Shape can be seen as an instrument of our mind to read the world. As graphic designers, we process these materials to present them in new ways. As scientists do, we rarely "invent" something, more often we analyse the surrounding and learn from it some laws and rules. That's why basic shapes can be considered the basis of our design process. They can be combined together to generate more complex shapes or even be the fundamental element to build a structural grid. Circle, square, triangle are something almost innate and, due to their simplicity, they are the potential base to build almost everything.

Happycentro

The three basic shapes — circle, square and triangle — have always been the basis for creation. In their form lies the original source of creativity and inspiration. They are the main components of the most iconic symbols made by men, and the foundation of a symbolic world. The three of them in the purest form can be used in design for a pragmatic approach, but can become so complex without losing their meaning that lies at the heart of aesthetic perception.

"Form follows function"

With no aim to compare favourably with the rest of basic geometric forms, the circumference is, without any doubt, the most special one. Because it's soft, thin, light and homogeneous. It's kind, sweet and delicate; moderate, balanced, subtle and evenly comfortable. For all these reasons, it's the most relaxed form and the one that gives more visual peace.

The circumference is the geometric metaphor for what it is democratic, as all its points have the same privileges — for all being equidistant from its centre — and therefore, any possible hierarchy is removed. Circumference suggests equality.

With no beginning and no ending, it shows how the infinite is something to tend to and thus, it becomes in a reference, something to admire. It represents purity, as it does not have any fissure nor mistakes. The only circumference can represent something unachievable: perfection.

Face.

Lo Siento

Another Land

Collective EP sleeves design for different artists under Border Community Recordings playing on bright yet minimalistic drawings. Already a beauty individually, the three designs are meant to fit together with the fourth (upcoming) for a larger picture of "Another Land".

Design: Jack Featherstone / Client: Border Community Recordings

Illustration series as a personal attempt to explore optical techniques. Here, Clouds rebuilds the gaseous body of clouds with a little bit of solidity, colour and shape.

Design: Jack Featherstone

Free will.

Agents have the ability to make choices. Individuals can be held morally accountable for
their actions. An omnipotent divinity does not assert its power over the will and choices of
individuals.

Solipsism.

Knowledge of anything outside one's own specific mind is unjustified. The external world
and other minds cannot be known and might not exist.

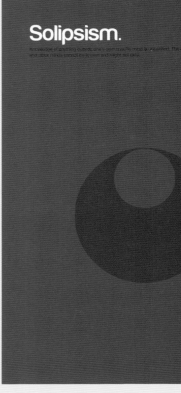

Determinism.

Events within a given paradigm are bound by causality in such a way that any state of an
object or event is determined by prior states. Every type of event, including human
behaviour, decision, and action is causally determined by previous events.

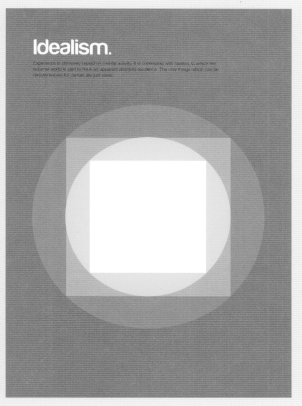

Idealism.

Experience is ultimately based on mental activity. It is contrasted with realism, in which the external world is said to have an apparent absolute existence. The only things which can be directly known for certain are just ideas.

Philographics

Philographics is a graphic journal of modern philosophy, where philosophical theories such as "absolutism" and "Idealism" were expressed as visual sensations. Focus was maintained using only simple colour combinations and shapes to compile the collection.

Design: Genís Carreras

Existentialism.

Individual is solely responsible for giving his or her own life meaning and for living that life passionately and sincerely, dealing with his or her conditions, emotions, actions, responsibilities, and thoughts.

Relativism.

Points of view have no absolute truth or validity, having only relative, subjective value according to differences in perception and consideration. Principles and ethics are regarded as applicable in only limited context.

Pixel

one
three two
two five six
four zero nine six

two
eight

six four
one zero two four

1/150

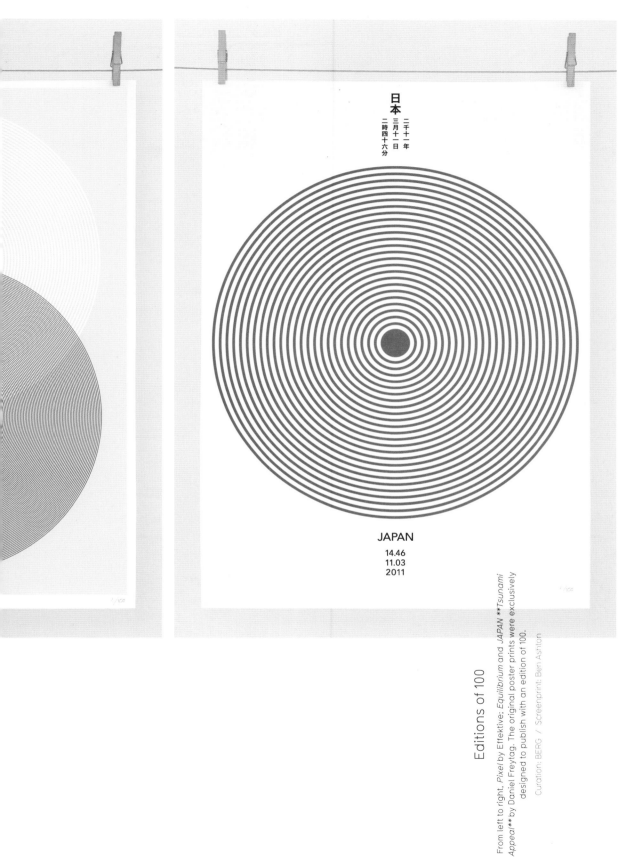

日本 二千十一年 三月十一日 二時四十六分

JAPAN

14.46
11.03
2011

Editions of 100

From left to right, *Pixel* by Effektive; *Equilibrium* and *JAPAN **Tsunami Appeal*** by Daniel Freytag. The original poster prints were exclusively designed to publish with an edition of 100.

Curation: BERG / Screenprint: Ben Ashton

MADE

Name and identity scheme for Leeds College of Art's annual pop-up shop where design graduates and undergraduates set out their work for sale. The name 'MADE' constructed on a multisegmented grid restated the event's focus on craft and artistry.

Design: Carl Holderness / Client: Leeds College of Art

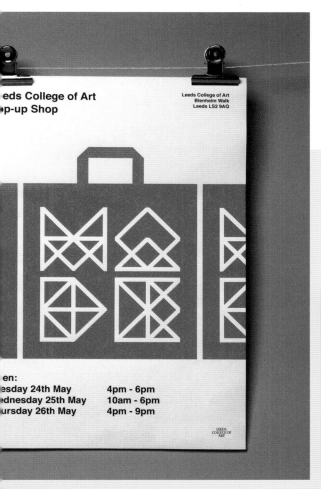

**eds College of Art
p-up Shop**

Leeds College of Art
Blenheim Walk
Leeds LS2 9AQ

en:
esday 24th May   4pm - 6pm
dnesday 25th May   10am - 6pm
ursday 26th May   4pm - 9pm

LEEDS
COLLEGE OF
ART

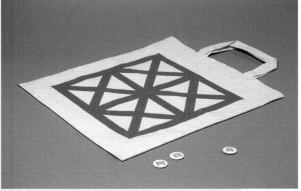

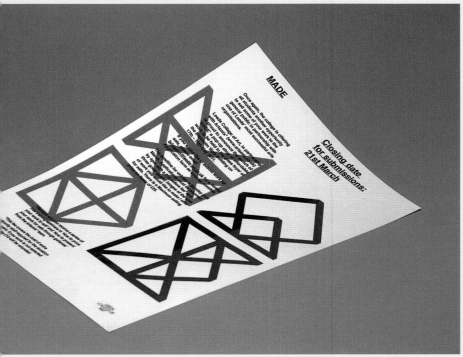

MADE

Closing date
for submissions:
21st March

The Salopian Inn

Identity for a culinary icon in the suburb of Adelaide stresses its half-timbered architecture with bold patterns and a black-and-white colour scheme. Its name honoured the architectural style's origin in Shropshire, the UK.

Design: Parallax Design / Client: The McLaren Vale Beer Company

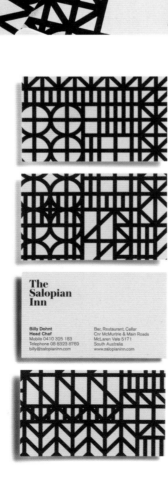

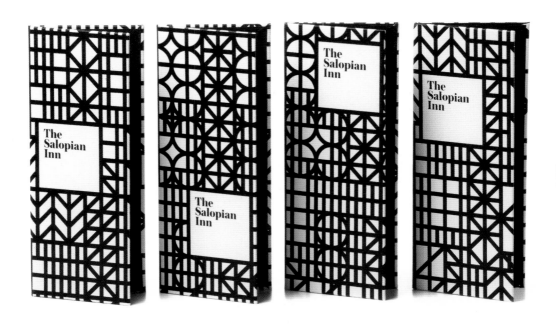

Feito com Vinil Identity

Meaning "Made With Vinyl", Feito Com Vinil's expertise in manufacturing vinyl decorations is as clear as day. Its playful and made-to-order aspect are further implied in its identity system, made of three graphic stamps and translucent inks.

Design: We Work For Knowledge / Client: Feito com Vinil

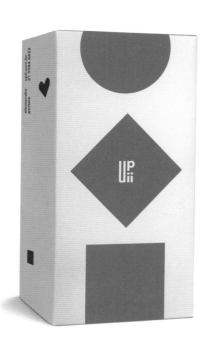

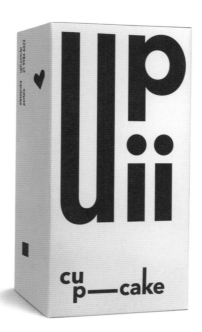

Upii Cupcakes Identity

Tiny discs, strokes, stars and hearts — the small shapes refer to the hearty additions in celebrations and on Upii's cupcakes. The idea is also communicated through a range of candy colours on Upii's promotional items and business cards.

Design: Rejane Dal Bello / Client: Upii

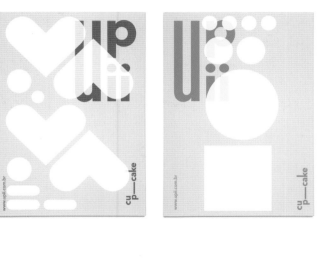

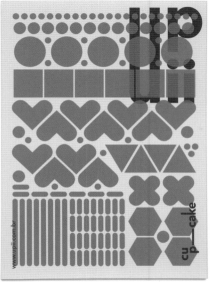

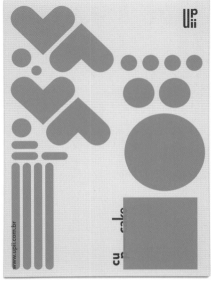

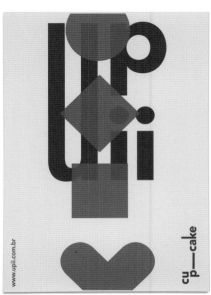

sa——bores

cupcakes de chocolate

UPII Brigadeiro	R$ 4,80
UPII Chocolate	R$ 4,50
UPII Chocolate Branco	R$ 4,80
UPII Nutella	R$ 5,30
UPII Floresta Negra	R$ 5,30

cupcakes de frutas

UPII Maça e Aveia	R$ 5,30
UPII Morango	R$ 5,30

cupcakes de frutas secas

UPII Amêndoa	R$ 5,30
UPII Nozes	R$ 5,30
UPII Natal	R$ 5,30

cupcakes variados

UPII Negresco	R$ 5,30
UPII Bis	R$ 5,30
UPII Beijinho	R$ 4,50
UPII Doce de Leite	R$ 4,50

MASSA DE CHOCOLATE OU MASSA DE BAUNILHA

DECORAÇÃO BÁSICA COM CONFEITOS DIVERSOS PREÇO INCLUÍDO

DECORAÇÃO COM PASTA AMERICANA, ACRÉSCIMO QUE VARIAM ENTRE R$0,70 À R$1,30

ANTECEDÊNCIA DO PEDIDO MÍNIMO DE 3 DIAS.

QUANTIDADE ACIMA DE 50 ENTRAR EM CONTATO PELO TEL OU E-MAIL.

UPII atende a todos os tipos de públicos e eventos, desde festas de aniversários, casamentos, chás e reuniões, até alguns eventos mais restritos.

UPII também segue um calendário anual de festividades, que você pode encontrar neste site.
Faça sua festa com essas pequenas delícias.

Encomende já o seu

(21) 9984 4422
www.upii.com.br

Up
ii
cu
p—cake
2011
sa
bores
festa

upii.com.br 21 9984 4422

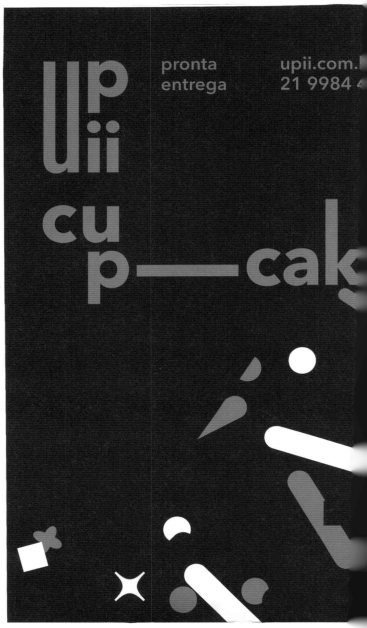

Up
ii
cu
p—cak

pronta
entrega

upii.com.
21 9984 4

cu
p—cake
Up
ii
R$ 4,0
sa
bores

upii.com.br 21 9984 4422

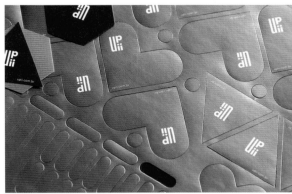

calendário de festa

cu p—cake

calendário de festa

cu p—cake

calendário de festa

PÁSCOA

24.04

DIA DAS
MÃES
♥
08.05

DIA DOS
NAMORADOS
♥
12.05

FESTA
JUNINA/JULHINA
🏮
24.06

HALLOWEEN
🦇
31.11

083

A UPII atende a todos os tipos
de públicos e eventos,
desde festas de aniversários,
casamentos, chás e reuniões,
até alguns eventos mais
restritos.

A UPII também segue um
calendário anual de festividades, que você pode encontrar
neste site.
Faça sua festa com essas
pequenas delícias.

Encomende já o seu

(21) 9984 4422
www.upii.com.br

A UPII atende a todos os tipos
de públicos e eventos,
desde festas de aniversários,
casamentos, chás e reuniões,
até alguns eventos mais
restritos.

A UPII também segue um
calendário anual de festividades, que você pode encontrar
neste site.
Faça sua festa com essas
pequenas delícias.

Encomende já o seu

(21) 9984 4422
www.upii.com.br

A UPII atende a todos os tipos
de públicos e eventos,
desde festas de aniversários,
casamentos, chás e reuniões,
até alguns eventos mais
restritos.

A UPII também segue um
calendário anual de festividades, que você pode encontrar
neste site.
Faça sua festa com essas
pequenas delícias.

Encomende já o seu

(21) 9984 4422
www.upii.com.br

deVega Medien Corporate Identity

New visual identity for German printer, deVega Medien. Circles being much the same as a
close-up halftone pattern translates deVega's capacity for fine printing and environmentally-
friendly productions in its corporate green, blue and silver.

Design: Keller Maurer Design / Client: deVega Medien GmbH

085

Achieve the Impossible

A campaign to beat the drum for Fedrigoni's paper selection tool called 'Imaginative Colours'. A tilted polygonal puncture centring every page of the booklets realise four Penrose shapes, as a perfect model of "achieve the impossible" in real life.

Design: William Cundall / Client: YCN Student Awards 2012

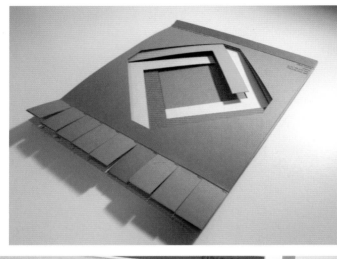

SIRIO COLOR
Bright Yellow
/m² 90,115,140,
70,210,350,480

SIRIO COLOR Verde
SIRIO COLOR
Pietra
g/m² 90,115,140,
170,210,350,480

SIRIO COLOR
Pietra
g/m 90,115,140
170,210,350,480

SIRIO COLOR
Pietra
g/m 90,115,140
170,210,350,480

HASSELL Poster 2010

2010 was a year of recognition for interdisciplinary design practice, HASSELL. The posters celebrated the signature forms extracted from HASSELL's award-winning projects, combined with several other projects as one idea, a process.

Design: Fabio Ongarato Design / Client: HASSELL

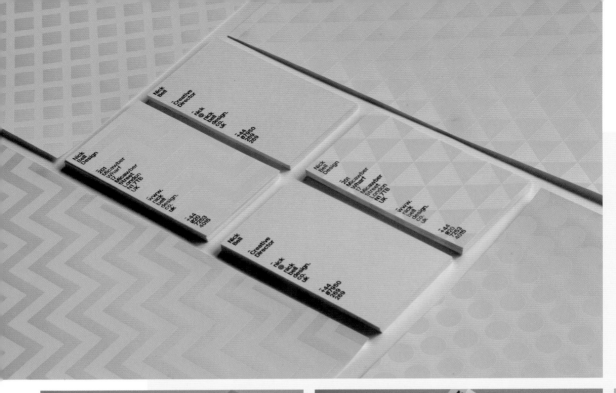

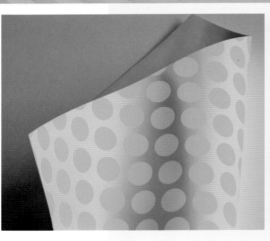

Nick Bell Design Identity & Stationery

Zestful and striking, Nick Bell Design's stationery concluded the team's qualities and exceptional visual communication strategies with 12 regular motifs and a vibrant fluorescent yellow ink. Letterhead details are only printed digitally on demand.

Design: Nick Bell Design / Photo & Printing: Generation Press

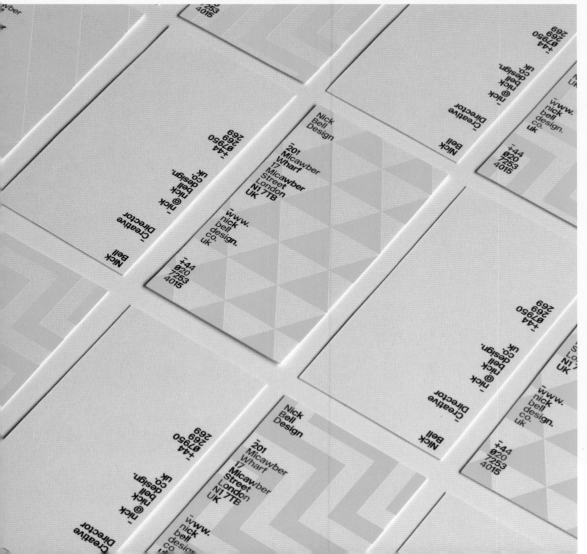

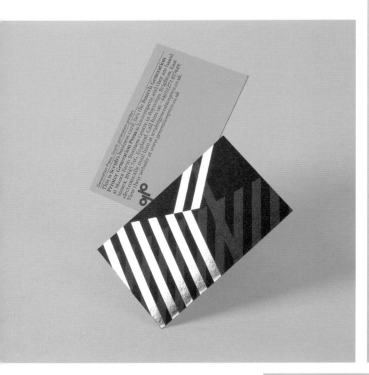

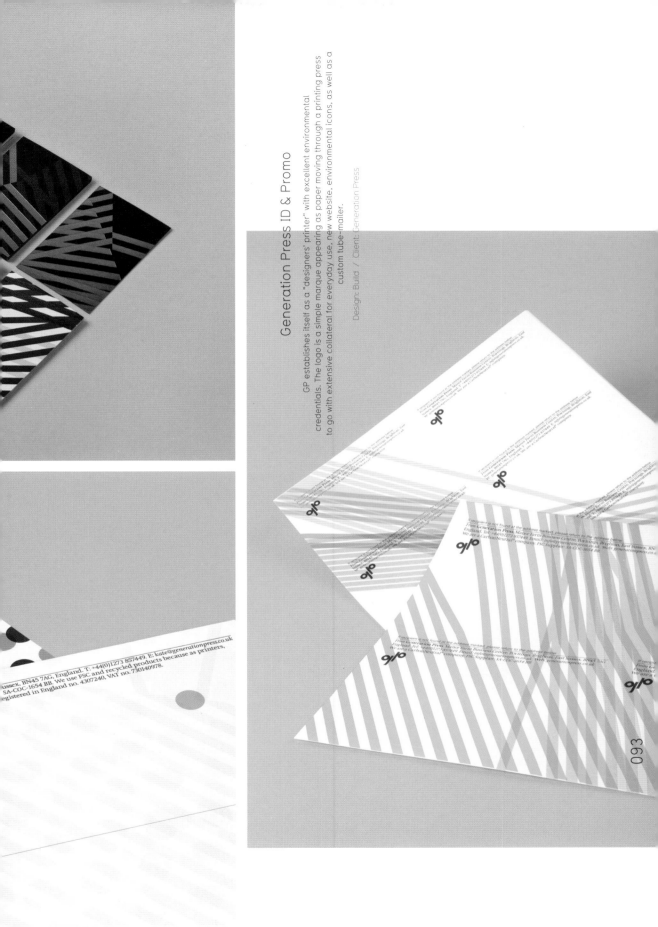

Generation Press ID & Promo

GP establishes itself as a "designers' printer" with excellent environmental credentials. The logo is a simple marque appearing as paper moving through a printing press to go with extensive collateral for everyday use, new website, environmental icons, as well as a custom tube-mailer.

Design: Build / Client: Generation Press

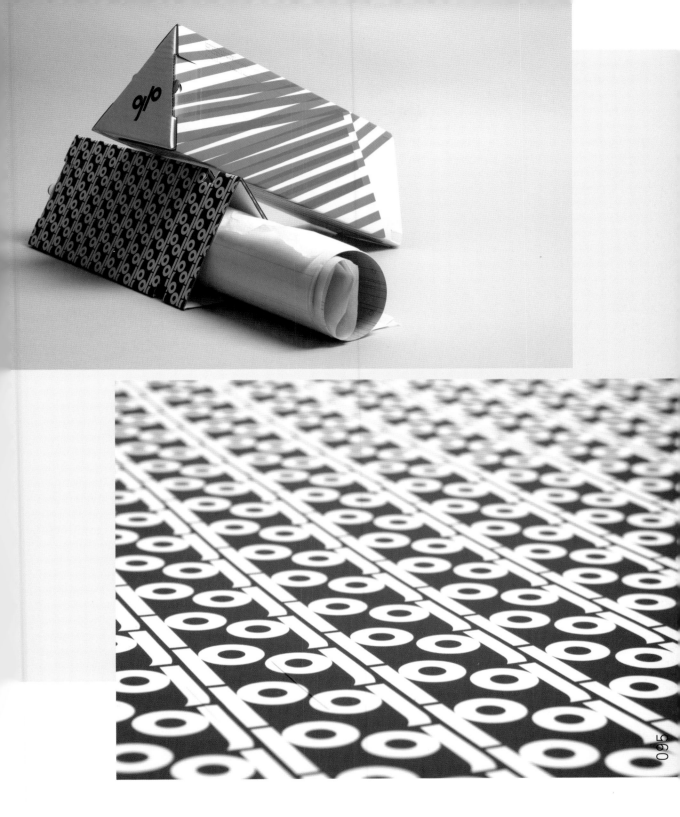

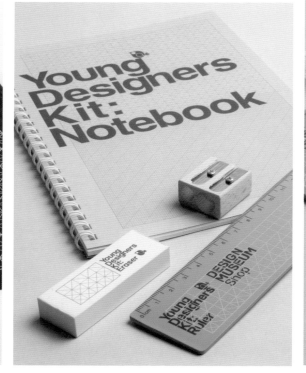

Design Museum Shop – Young Designers Kit

Stationery items aimed at younger visitors of the Design Museum in London. As well as inspiration, the items were also an exemplar of environmentally-conscious products, made with fully certified organic canvas, recycled CD cases, etc.

Design: Build / Client: Design Museum, London

097

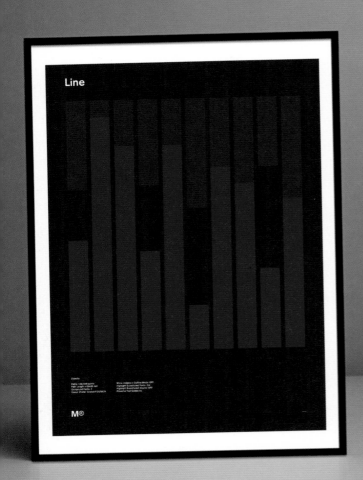

Geometry

An ongoing series of 1950/60's inspired posters that studies Armin Hofmann's output and creative styles, expressing modern ideas in geometric patterns. A line of words demonstrate how the composition can be presented in an alternative way.

Design: Mister

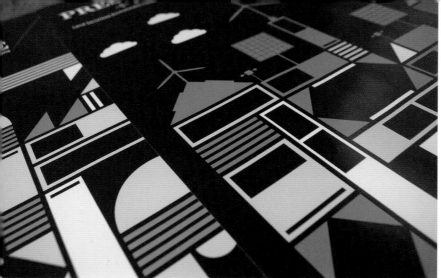

Past, Present & Future

The tritych explores environmental issues sprung from large scale urban developments at different points of time. Designed under the watchful eye of Michael Johnson of Johnson Banks, the posters were produced for a regular conference held by Land Securities.

Design: Teacake / Client: Land Securities

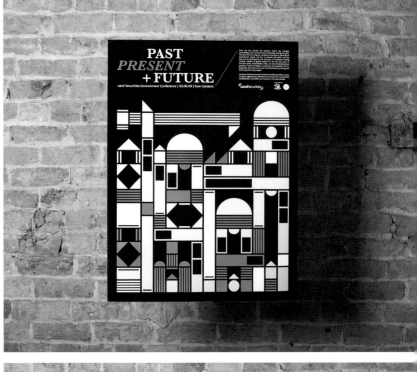

The Hall of Forgotten Fame

An ongoing portrait series first initiated to turn an evening gathering at Aviator into a surreal "Hall of Fame". The portraits imagined a selection of important characters whom might have stayed at the hotel. Shapes added a retro twist with a modern feel.

Design: Emily Forgot / Client: studio BKKR

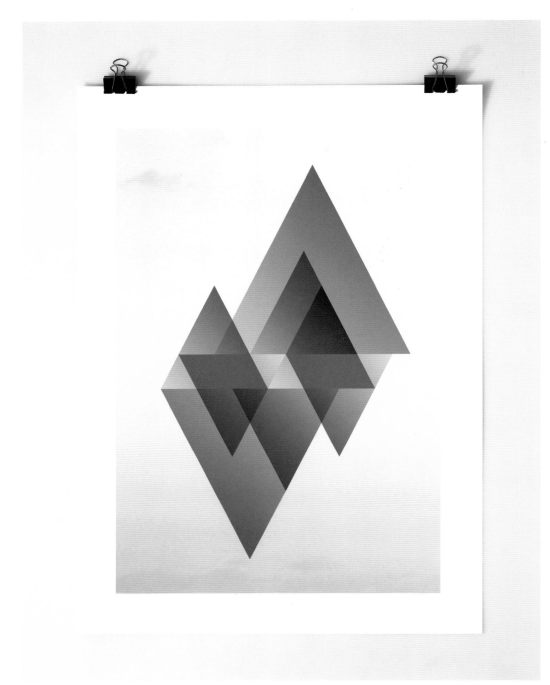

Format 1.0

An investigational poster series using overlapping and interlinking
shapes to produce larger dynamic forms.

Design: Motherbird

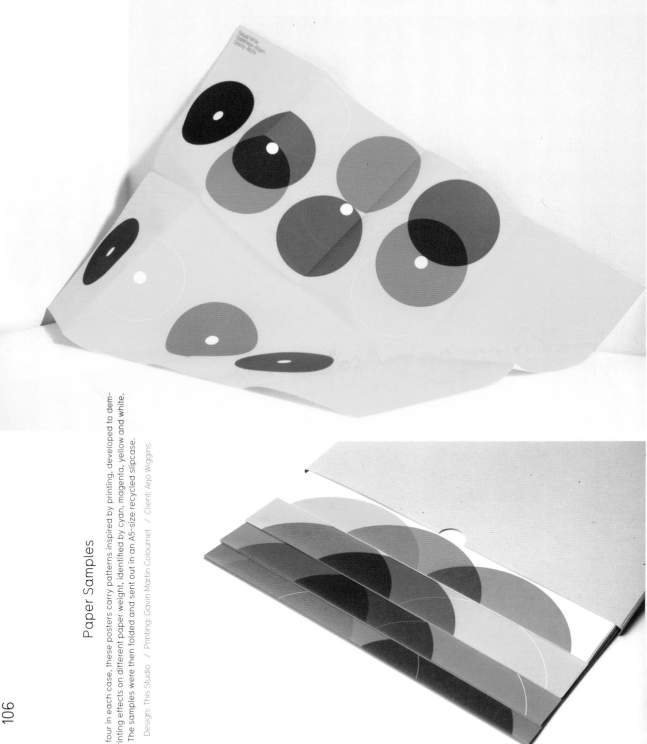

Paper Samples

Containing four in each case, these posters carry patterns inspired by printing, developed to demonstrate printing effects on different paper weight, identified by cyan, magenta, yellow and white. The samples were then folded and sent out in an A5-size recycled slipcase.

Design: This Studio / Printing: Gavin Martin Colournet / Client: Arjo Wiggins

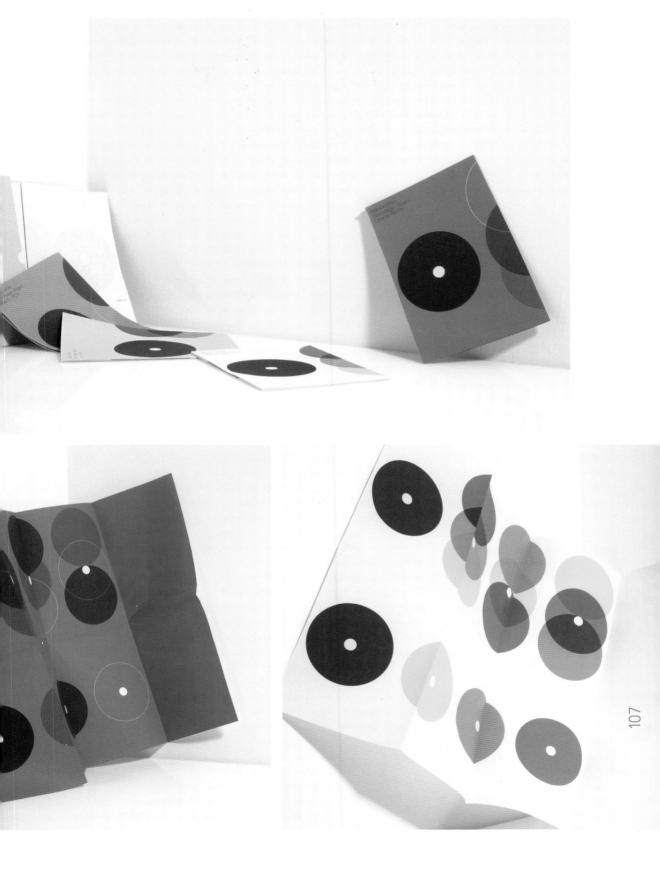

Subb-An: Take You Back

Album cover for British artist Subb-An, echoing the title by pulling aesthetics from his last release as an actual step back in time. The images conceptualised time travel, as well as the retro aspect of the disc.

Design: Cina Associates / Client: Ghostly International

A limited print that symbolises the duality of music and design commentary on Bridging the Gap and commemorates the blog's second birthday. The metallic print was manually silkscreened by Loren at Loligo.

Design: Ross Gunter / Client: Bridging the Gap

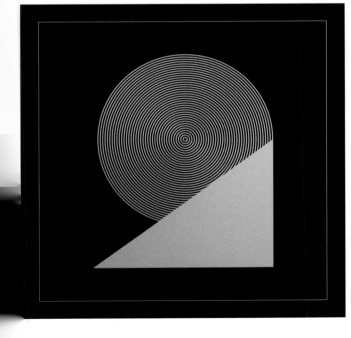

Archphoto 2.0

Archphoto 2.0 is an Italian review of architecture and design issues related to local public affairs. Its issue zero studied the changes within the society between 1861 and 2011, starting with an attack on the government's failure at preserving heritage.

Design: ARTIVA DESIGN / Client: plug in editions

Lezioni di Paesaggio

Publication and poster introducing a collection of writings and pictures on landscapes of northern Italy with respect to architectural and artistic heritage. The hollow circle was an allusion to the connection between open and closed space.

Design: ARTIVA DESIGN / Client: plug_in editions

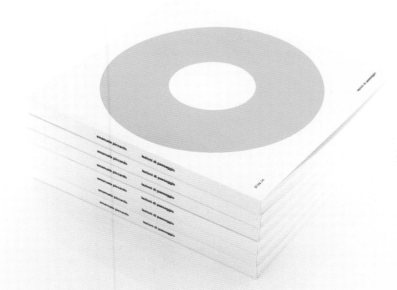

Müller-Brockmann
Hofmann
Crouwel

swiss style
—
the peak of poster design

During the 1950s, a design emerged from Switzerland
and Germany that has been called Swiss Design,
or more appropriately, the International Typographic Style.
The objective clarity of this design movement won converts
throughout the world. It remained a major force for over two
decades, and its influence continues.

- Philip Meggs

3

Swiss Style: The Peak Of Poster

Restating the exhibition's theme, this catalogue gave a nod to the hallmarks of
Swiss Style and posters by Josef Müller-Brockmann, Armin Hofmann and Wim Crouwel. A mono-
chrome piece generated as either a positive print or a negative was
an added bonus to give away.

Design: Duane Dalton

swiss style
—
the peak of poster design

Müller-Brockmann
Hofmann
Crouwel

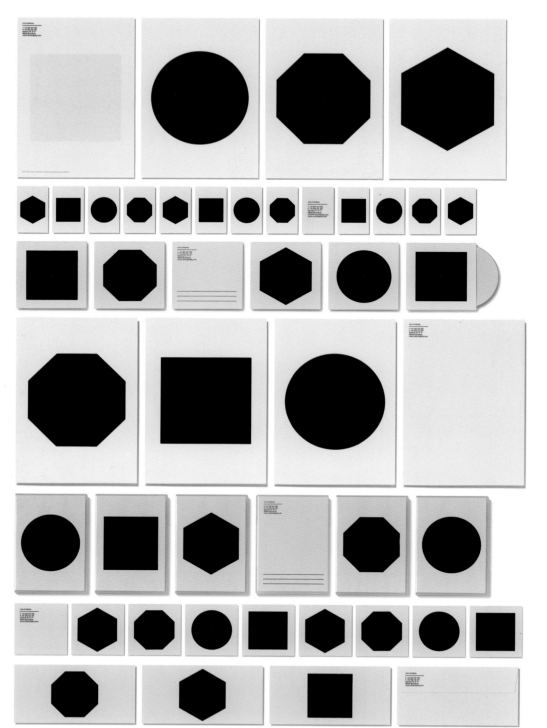

ruiz+company Identity

Using merely four geometric figures, in black on white with a humble typeface,
ruiz+company established a statement against gliding the lily. The shapes unspecifically
stood for "synthesis", "purity" and "conceptuality" that define their work.

Design: ruiz+company

Illustrations and booklets demonstrating ARTIVA's research into the possibility of creating simple modules as the foundations of ridiculous architectural designs. Three humble blocks were rendered, like a fresh take on the fabulous Lego bricks.

Design: ARTIVA DESIGN

▲ APPROVED™

Made in New York City	Hecho en la ciudad de Nueva York	Approved is a storefront for affordable graphic, product, and apparel design.	Approved es una tienda de productos de diseño gráfico, industrial y textil.
Graphic / Product / Apparel	Gráfica / Industrial / Textil	All items have been hand selected in order to provide you with affordable design-oriented products without compromising quality.	Todos los productos han sido seleccionados a mano para poder proveer productos de calidad y de buen diseño a precios accesibles.

Approved

Approved is an ongoing collaboration between apparel, industrial and graphic designers, who take triangles as the common language to create by various means. These posters speak of the group's true beliefs in creative freedom.

Design: Derek Kim / Client: Approved

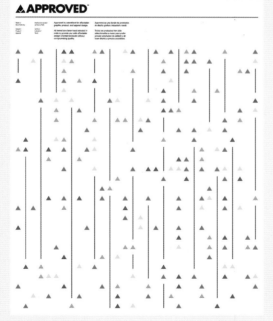

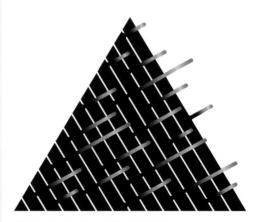

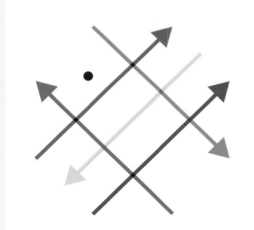

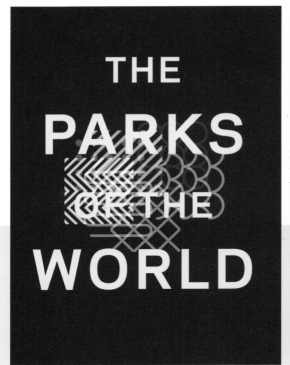

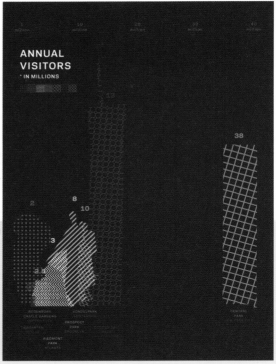

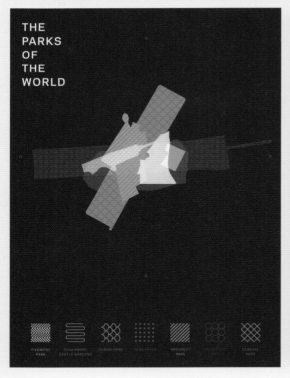

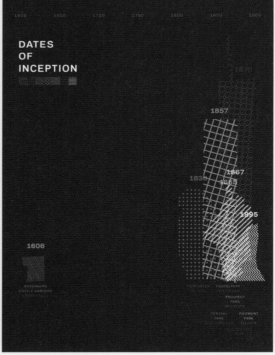

Parks Of The World

An illustration collection created as a visual memory of the urban parks that the designer has visited in 2011. The parks were compared in different aspects, including size, shape, number of annual visitors and date of inception.

THE
PARKS
OF
THE
WORLD

1,017
ACRES

843
ACRES

585
ACRES

520
ACRES

189
ACRES

120
ACRES

40
ACRES

ROSENBORG
CASTLE GARDENS
COPENHAGEN

VONDELPARK
AMSTERDAM

PIEDMONT
PARK
ATLANTA

TIERGARTEN
BERLIN

PROSPECT
PARK
BROOKLYN

CENTRAL
PARK
NEW YORK CITY

GOLDEN GATE
PARK
SAN FRANCISCO

Season Carpet

Season Carpet is developed to imitate the nature's ability to change, just like flower blooms in spring and snow falls in the cold days. Responsive to temperatures, these prototypes demonstrate a clear view of colour change in a tricolour braided design.

Design: Siren Elise Wilhelmsen / Material Sponsor & Thermocoromic Colour: Matsui International Company Inc.

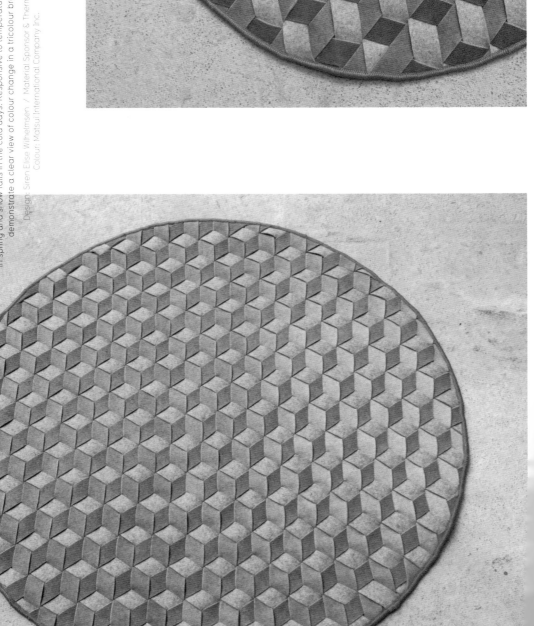

ALEATORIC SERIES

Started as an open-ended experimentation, these compounds are a random fusion of Shlian's organic formations and Cina's abstractionist canvas work. By sticking to one form, the result was an emergent system of ordering the dischord.

Design: Matthew Shlian & Michael Cina / Client: Ghostly International 2012 / Photo: Cullen Stephenson

Finca Cucó Wine Packaging

"Cucó" is typical of Priorat region, with a small circle entrance located on the cultivated land. The graphic is a synthesis of the stone cottage and the wine's guaranteed quality produced from Montsant, a Spanish Denominación de Origen.

Design: Atipus / Client: Celler El Masroig

Pillar Box / Morse Code Packaging

Named after Henry Hill who once owned the Adelaide-Melbourne mail coach, the wine operator founded their brand around "postage". While Pillar Box calls up the virtues of patience and waiting, Morse Code honoured the craft of postal telegraphists.

Design: Parallax Design / Client: Henry's Drive Vignerons

RAJA LALA
DEEN DAYAL

Raja Lala Deen Dayal Identity

Marrying a camera's aperture with a brilliant's facets, the logo likens Raja Deen Dayal, a 19th century legendary Indian photographer, to a 'gem'. His exquisite record of British India was particularly spotlighted as a marketing gimmick in his brand identity.

Design: Siddharth Khandelwal / Client: Raja Lala Deendayal Family Trust

124

RAJA LALA
DEEN DAYAL

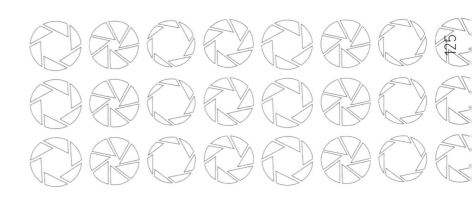

125

When an idea begins and comes to fruition, precision and attention to detail is where the square undoubtably becomes one of the most useful tools a designer can have.

Although metaphorically it might suggest uniformity and monotony, square sets a simple standard of rules which can be broken. Where complex layout decisions and balance in the distribution of objects are made, all are held true to the strong and perfect square form.

Carl Holderness

Simple geometric structures have always been at the core of my art. There is something intrinsically beautiful about the simplification of forms. What I love about geometric shapes is that playing with them is like playing with Lego bricks. As a kid, I was obsessed with Lego; the modularity of these bricks allowed me to create anything I envisioned from scratch. In spite of the fact that certain sets were to be assembled for a specific scenario, it also allowed me to create anything within my own imagination and this creative freedom is exactly what I'm obsessed about. The same goes for geometric shapes; It creates a nice modular system where you can lay down standard and familiar shapes to create a bigger picture in a beautiful and simple way.

Derek Kim

Triangles have really been popular for the last years, almost like a "sell out". Nevertheless they are timeless, simple yet fascinating shapes. Especially if you turn it upside down, this ordinary move gives it a totally different impression, making it more threatening, almost aggressive.

A really impressive variation based on triangle is the Penrose Triangle, which is an impossible object. It's still pretty simple. Only with a few more lines, the shape gains a third dimension in an unreal way.

Ice Cream For Free™

I have no interest in exploring shape purely as form. Used in conjunction with composition and colour forms become emotions, memories and light. For me this is when any primitive shape has the potential to cause suffering, unease, happiness, love or passion. There is such romance attached to paintings in which caused an effect on an individual. This is what I would like to achieve. When discussing a single shape the rectangle for me has the widest scope of use to create this emotional response. When used as a modest thin stroke to convey structure and delicacy or when used with almost equal proportions to give dominance and power.

Christopher Gray

Since my childhood there is something disturbing in my mind that from time to time comes up and then just disappears. It gets stuck in my head and is simply not leaving me. By and large, it reflects the full force of the ways that our senses perceive the world around us and incorporate them in ourselves – but just as well to give again the views to the outside.
I'm talking fortunately not of the evil in me, but about the simple and legendary sounds and images of the Tetris – 'Game Boy' Game and thus actually the first indication of my dependence on geometric figures and simple colours in my work.

Viktor Matic

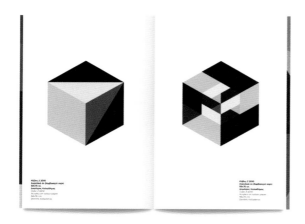

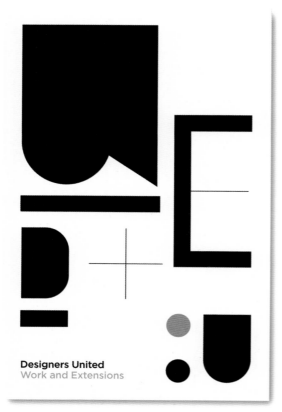

Designers United
Work and Extensions

Designers United Work & Extensions Catalogue 2011

A 380-page monograph on Designers United's projects for exhibition, *The Gestalt Effect / Work & Extensions of Designers United*, at Macedonian Museum of Contemporary Art, curated by art historian Thouli Misirloglou. The catalogue has six books with different focuses, including forms and logos, and contributor text.

Design: Designers United

Emergency-Congress 2012

Designed for the first Panhellenic Congress on Emergency Prehospital Care in Greece, the bilingual scientific program visually brings out two main aspects of the job. While the organic cross and triangle create the tension, an exposed book spine stitching takes reference to an open wound with red surgical thread.

Design: Designers United / Client: Pan-Hellenic Congress 2012

Emergency

1o ΠΑΝΕΛΛΗΝΙΟ
ΣΥΝΕΔΡΙΟ
ΕΠΕΙΓΟΥΣΑΣ
ΠΡΟΝΟΣΟΚΟΜΕΙΑΚΗΣ
ΦΡΟΝΤΙΔΑΣ
ΜΕ ΔΙΕΘΝΗ ΣΥΜΜΕΤΟΧΗ

1st PAN-HELLENIC
CONGRESS
ON EMERGENCY
PREHOSPITAL CARE
WITH INTERNATIONAL
PARTICIPATION

EEEPF.GR

THESSALONIKI / GREECE
27–28.04.2012

THE MET HOTEL

131

Anúncio M20

M2's 20 years of devotion to graphics and art as a print house was celebrated on press ads and cards. Indicating "good partnerships add value", print quality was stressed through a colourful pattern constructed from a deconstructed "M20" wherein "20 ANOS (20 years)" subtly submerged as blind-embossed types.

Design: MAGA Atelier / Client: M2 – Artes Gráficas

Build Things

A graphical support to the statement, 'We must build to become built'. Shapes were taken as building toy blocks, in primary colours to graphically reinforce the structure and childhood memories of building with toy bricks.

Design: Joe Joiner

Rua Adriano Canas nº 19 2740-003
Porto Salvo, Portugal
Tel.: (+351) 214218600
e-mail: info@mood.pt

www.mood.pt

LAMP DESIGN
& LIGHTING CONCEPT

Filipa Maia
Designer
filipamaia@mood.pt

MOOD®
Lamp Design & Lighting Concept

Rua Adriano Canas nº 19 2740-003
Porto Salvo, Portugal
(+351) 214218600
info@mood.pt

www.mood.pt

Rita Muralha
Arquitecta
(+351) 919 601 737
ritamuralha@mood.pt

MOOD®
Lamp Design & Lighting Concept

Rua Adriano Canas nº 19 2740-003
Porto Salvo, Portugal
(+351) 214218600
info@mood.pt

www.mood.pt

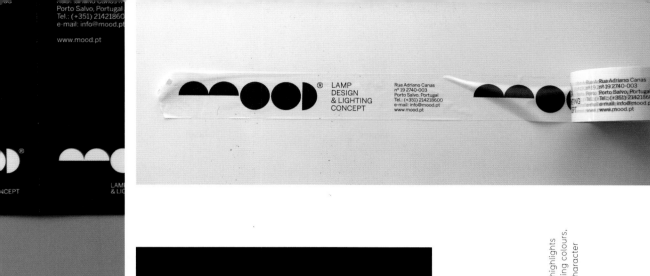

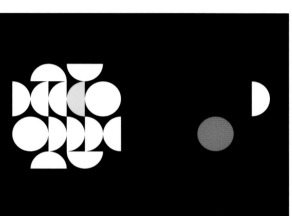

MOOD Identity

Distinguishing their lighting fixtures with sculptural qualities, Mood's visual identity highlights "modularity" as the mentality of Mood's lamp design. 'Diversity' is explored by combining colours, printing and circles as the primary element, creating distinctive movements and character in the brand's logo, catalogues and packaging design.

Design: MAGA Atelier / Client: MOOD–Lamp Design & Lighting Concept

PAPER OBJECTS

Happycentro's self-promotional project was founded on their particular love for paper, texture, handicraft and halftoning. The sculptures were set off with a diagram, outlining its original structure and form as a square paper with assorted patterns.

Design: Happycentro

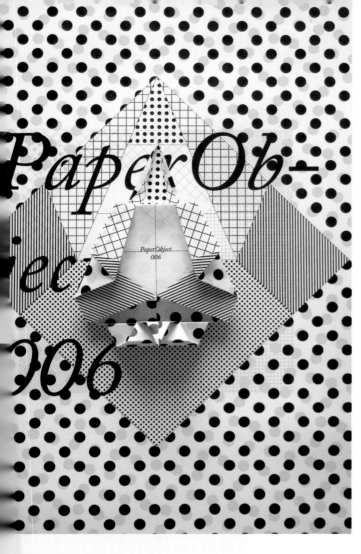

Paper Ob-
ject
006

Everyday Geometry

A celebration of everyday objects. Stationery and tools were deliberately destructed or set to create a visual link with the geometry already embraced in them.

Design: Carl Kleiner

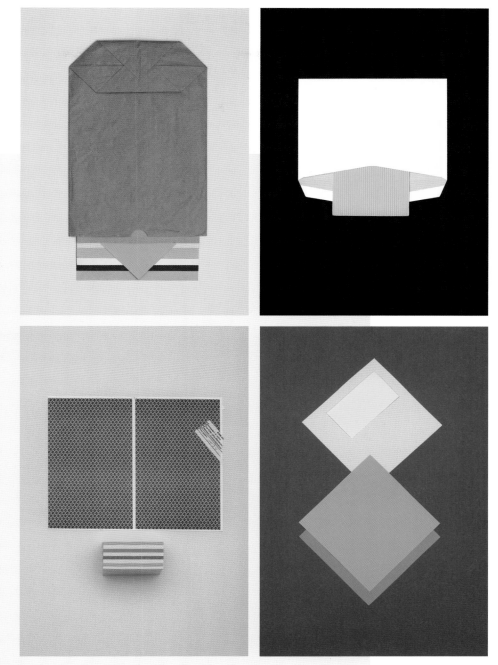

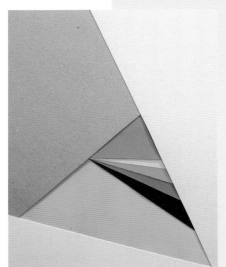
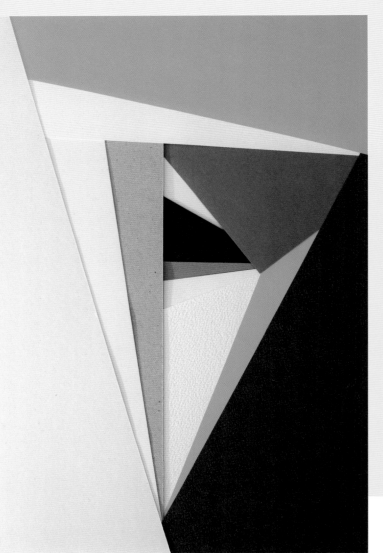

The Bærtling Wannabe

A geometrical study in colour with homage to Olle Bærtling's 'open form' geometric paintings. Kleiner's version is a swirl of colour paper illustrating triangles with their rims.

Design: Carl Kleiner

Reproductions

Graphic and abstracted edition of selected famous paintings, such as Munch's *Scream*, with shapes and simplified shades. The collection was aimed to cast a different understanding of renowned art paintings and give individuals an opportunity to rediscover the referenced art pieces.

Design: Christopher Gray

143

Expanded View / Plastic Messiah

Two graphically full-to-bursting collage composed of found images,
acrylic, spray paints, etc. On this page is *Expanded View*, originally created
for Goolsby's first solo show in Los Angeles entitled "Tomorrow's Nothing".
On facing page is *Plastic Messiah*, also with ink and aluminum foil,
intensified with a patterned fabric base.

Design: Clark Goolsby

DIPSIE AS WELL / THIS IS NOW

Illustrations with aesthetics found in a collage of shapes, found images, patterns and bright colours. On this page is digital patchwork for fictional record label, DIPSIE AS WELL. On the next is *THIS IS NOW*, composed and contributed as one of the world's most influencial elements on modern aesthetics in visual arts.

Design: ICE CREAM FOR FREE™ / Client: Oh Yeah Studio (THIS IS NOW)

DIPSIE AS WELL

Digital patchwork for record sleeves released by fictional record label, DIPSIE AS WELL. The packaging artwork offered an alternative to traditional sleeve design, joining up photographs, paintings, graphic patterns and 3D digital renderings of contrasting styles.

Design: ICE CREAM FOR FREE™

143

142

ODD SERIES

An illustration series defiling the common conception of femininity that is likely reckoned as "odd portraits" with a frown. Invited and commissioned to put on the artist marketplace – artisticly and sold as limited framed prints, the illustrations were reproduced using German etching papers and archival materials.

Design: ICE CREAM FOR FREE™ / Client: Magnolia Box

Dear Life Alphabet

Looking for a simple happy life with less hard times, Machado initiated these alphabets in its most basic yet legible forms with every exquisite details eschewed. The piece ended up in a personal letter to life, begging for kindness in a lighthearted way.

Design: João Ricardo Machado

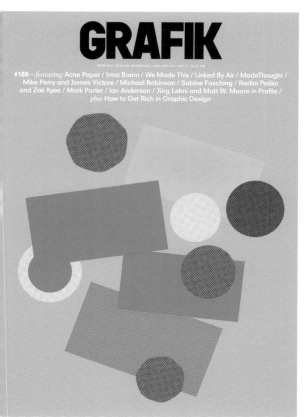

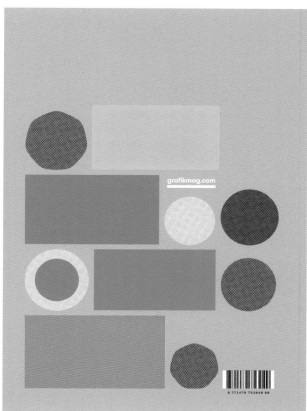

Cover art taking shapes as the simplified forms of objects. Above is *Money Talks,* cover illustration for *Grafik's* relaunch issue probing the business side of graphic design. At the bottom is a modular identity system for Museum Metadata Exchange, launched by Sydney's Powerhouse Museum to promote access to its collection data.

Art Direction: Michael Bojkowski (Grafik) / Design: Heath Killen / Client: Grafik, Powerhouse Museum

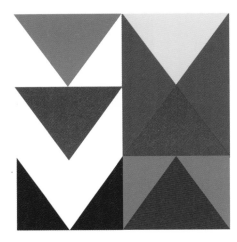

A sample and exploration of balanced colours for paper merchant, GF smith. Bold and clean geometric shapes were deliberately used as a structural reference for colour card users to identify harmony or contrasts between primary, secondary and tertiary colours in print.

Design: Chantelle Kamolo McLean · Client: GF Smith

Colorplan is GF Smith's flagship range of 56 coloured papers with extensive combinations of weights, duplexing, embossings and envelopes.

Colorplan is GF Smith's flagship range of 56 coloured papers with extensive combinations of weights, duplexing, embossings and envelopes.

GF Smith Colorplan: The Student Edition
ary Colours

mith
wood Street,
OHL

Email
Info@gfsmith.com

Telephone
01482 323 503

Facsimile
01482 223 174

GF Smith Colorplan: The Student Edition
Complimentary Colours

GF Smith
Lockwood Street,
Hull, HU2 OHL

Email
Info@gfsmith.com

Telephone
01482 323 503

Facsimile
01482 223 174

Colorplan is GF Smith's flagship range of 56 coloured papers with extensive combinations of weights, duplexing, embossings and envelopes.

GF Smith Colorplan: The Student Edition
Receding Colours

GF Smith
Lockwood Street,
Hull, HU2 OHL

Email
Info@gfsmith.com

Telephone
01482 323 503

Facsimile
01482 223 174

GF Smith Colorplan: The
Tertiary Colours

GF Smith
Lockwood Street,
Hull, HU2 OHL

GF Smith Coloplan: The Student Edition
Primary Colours

GF Smith, Lockwood Street,
Hull, HU2 0HL

Email
Info@gfsmith.com

Telephone
01482 323 503

Facsimile
01482 223 174

Coloplan is GF Smith's flagship range of 56 coloured papers with extensive combinations of weights, duplexing, embossing and envelopes.

GF Smith Coloplan: The Student Edition
Juxtaposition

GF Smith, Lockwood Street,
Hull, HU2 0HL

Email
Info@gfsmith.com

Telephone
01482 323 503

Facsimile
01482 223 174

Coloplan is GF Smith's flagship range of 56 coloured papers with extensive combinations of weights, duplexing, embossing and envelopes.

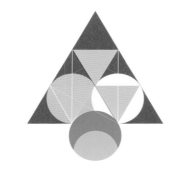

GF Smith Coloplan: The Student Edition
Primary Colours

GF Smith
Lockwood Street,
Hull
HU2 0HL

Email
Info@gfsmith.com

Telephone
01482 323 503

Facsimile
01482 223 174

Coloplan is GF Smith's flagship range of 56 coloured papers with extensive combinations of weights, duplexing, embossing and envelopes.

GF Smith Coloplan: The Student Edition
Complementary Colours

GF Smith
Lockwood Street,
Hull
HU2 0HL

Email
Info@gfsmith.com

Telephone
01482 323 503

Facsimile
01482 223 174

Coloplan is GF Smith's flagship range of 56 coloured papers with extensive combinations of weights, duplexing, embossing and envelopes.

---

56 coloured
ights, duplexing,

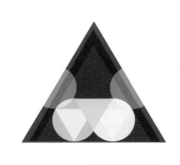

GF Smith Coloplan: The Student Edition
Advancing Colours

GF Smith
Lockwood Street,
Hull
HU2 0HL

Email
Info@gfsmith.com

Telephone
01482 323 503

Facsimile
01482 223 174

Coloplan is GF Smith's flagship range of 56 coloured papers with extensive combinations of weights, duplexing, embossing and envelopes.

GF Smith Coloplan: The Student Edition
Receding Colours

GF Smith
Lockwood Street,
Hull
HU2 0HL

Email
Info@gfsmith.com

Telephone
01482 323 503

Facsimile
01482 223 174

Coloplan is GF Smith's flagship range of 56 coloured papers with extensive combinations of weights, duplexing, embossing and envelopes.

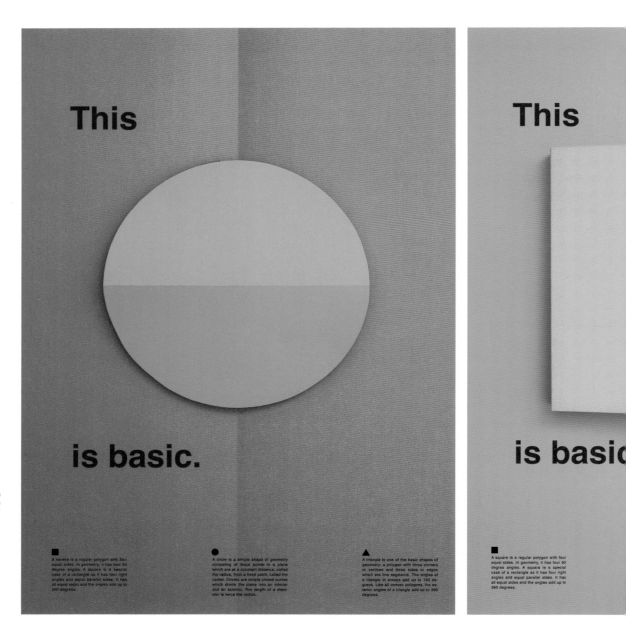

This

is basic.

■ A square is a regular polygon with four equal sides. In geometry, it has four 90 degree angles. A square is a special case of a rectangle as it has four right angles and equal parallel sides. It has all equal sides and the angles add up to 360 degrees.

● A circle is a simple shape of geometry consisting of those points in a plane which are at a constant distance, called the radius, from a fixed point, called the center. Circles are simple closed curves which divide the plane into an interior and an exterior. The length of a diameter is twice the radius.

▲ A triangle is one of the basic shapes of geometry; a polygon with three corners or vertices and three sides or edges which are line segments. The angles of a triangle always add up to 180 degrees. Like all convex polygons, the exterior angles of a triangle add up to 360 degrees.

This

is basic.

■ A square is a regular polygon with four equal sides. In geometry, it has four 90 degree angles. A square is a special case of a rectangle as it has four right angles and equal parallel sides. It has all equal sides and the angles add up to 360 degrees.

This Is Basic

This Is Basic explored infinity in the simplest matters. While planes, shadows, hues and reflections were in the subject, the idea was analysed at different levels through photos, pop-up posters and paper sculptures. The installation took place as part of exhibition, *Lift Off*, during Dutch Design Week 2008.

Design: Raw Color / Client: Freek Lomme (Onomatopee), Dave Keune

This

is basic.

▲ A triangle is one of the basic shapes of geometry: a polygon with three corners or vertices and three sides or edges which are line segments. The angles of a triangle in always add up to 180 degrees. Like all convex polygons, the exterior angles of a triangle add up to 360 degrees.

■ A square is a regular polygon with four equal sides. In geometry, it has four 90 degree angles. A square is a special case of a rectangle as it has four right angles and equal parallel sides. It has all equal sides and the angles add up to 360 degrees.

● A circle is a simple shape of geometry consisting of those points in a plane which are at a constant distance, called the radius, from a fixed point, called the center. Circles are simple closed curves which divide the plane into an interior and an exterior. The length of a diameter is twice the radius.

▲ A triangle is one of the basic shapes of geometry: a polygon with three corners or vertices and three sides or edges which are line segments. The angles of a triangle in always add up to 180 degrees. Like all convex polygons, the exterior angles of a triangle add up to 360 degrees.

Adventure into Design

Bursting into colourful blocks scattering in the air, the thrill of excitement visualised "Adventure into Design" as Billy Blue School of Design opened a campus in Melbourne. Handmade paper shape scenes were based around the Billy Blue values – thinking, making and connecting.

Design: Motherbird / Client: Billy Blue School of Design

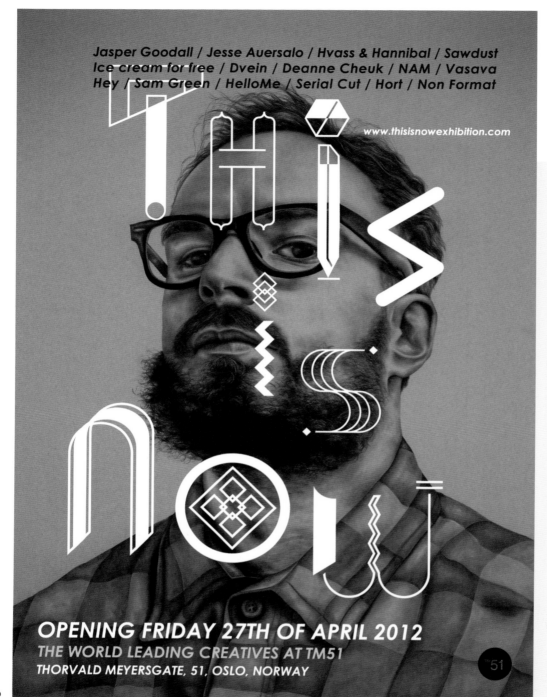

Jasper Goodall / Jesse Auersalo / Hvass & Hannibal / Sawdust
Ice cream for free / Dvein / Deanne Cheuk / NAM / Vasava
Hey / Sam Green / HelloMe / Serial Cut / Hort / Non Format

www.thisisnowexhibition.com

OPENING FRIDAY 27TH OF APRIL 2012
THE WORLD LEADING CREATIVES AT TM51
THORVALD MEYERSGATE, 51, OSLO, NORWAY

THIS IS NOW

"THIS IS NOW" indicates the great impact which prolific designers, illustrators and motion artists have on visual language today. Taking significant elements that represent the current semiotic drift, the posters introduce the event where poster art and motion graphics from 15 of the world's leading creatives would be on display.

Design: Oh Yeah Studio

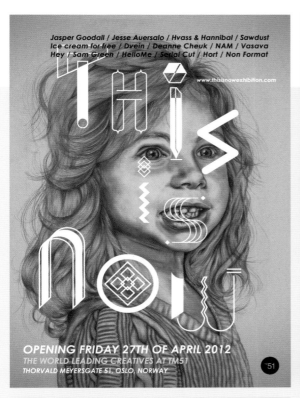

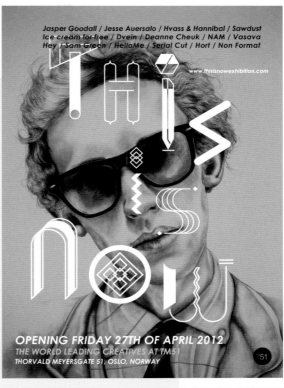

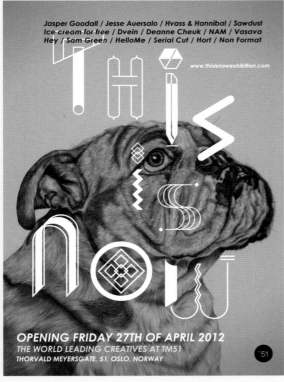

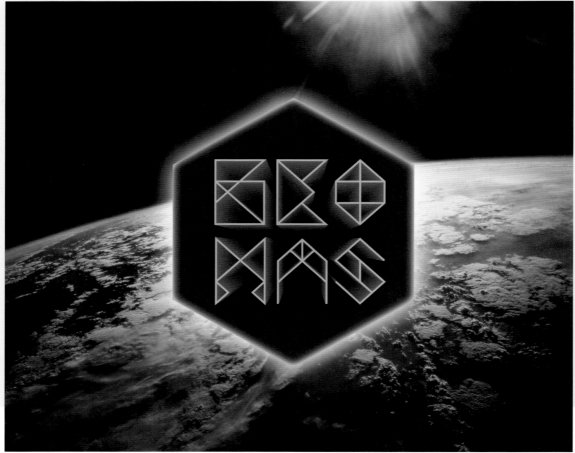

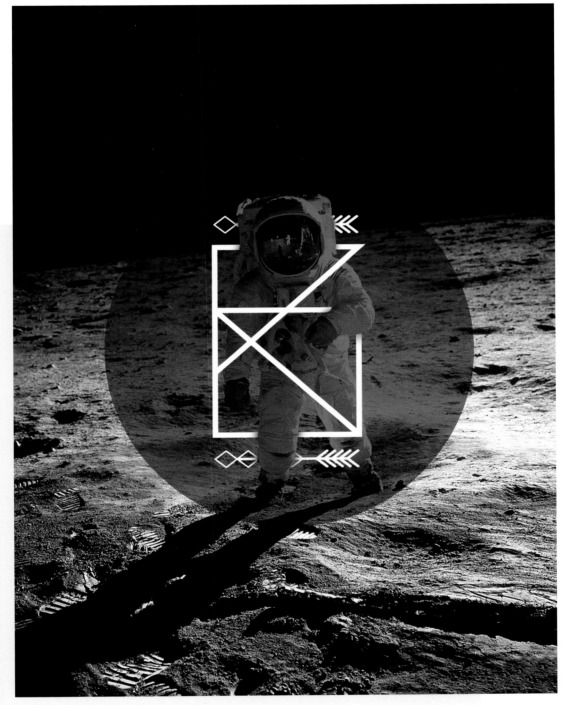

OLUMAS

Typographic design inspired by dubstep music, in particular, the first part of *Kill The Noise*. To Kelava, it was futuristic, bold, calculated and systematic. All alphabets, numbers and symbols were derived from the same sectioned grids that give the letters a geometric character.

Design: Josip Kelava

163

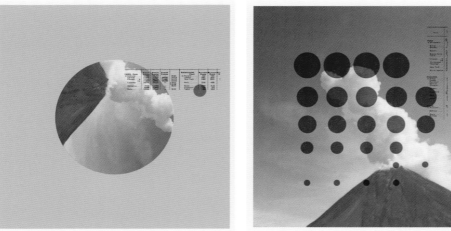

That Hesitation / Daylight and the Sun

Vintage artwork as Couceiro's response to day and night. On the left, *That Hesitation When Dawn Trembles and Night Pauses* picture relationships between day and night, light and darkness and their effect on emotions. *Daylight and the Sun* on facing page is a graphic project inspired by the scenes with the sun and light from Virginia Woolf's classic novel, *The Waves.*

Design: Cristiana Couceiro

POSITION;

10/19/25

1/6

2,939,517

8
mm.

No. 337

Back
Back
Forward
Punch
—
**Red
Boots**

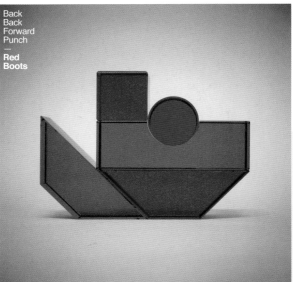

Back
Back
Forward
Punch
—
Always

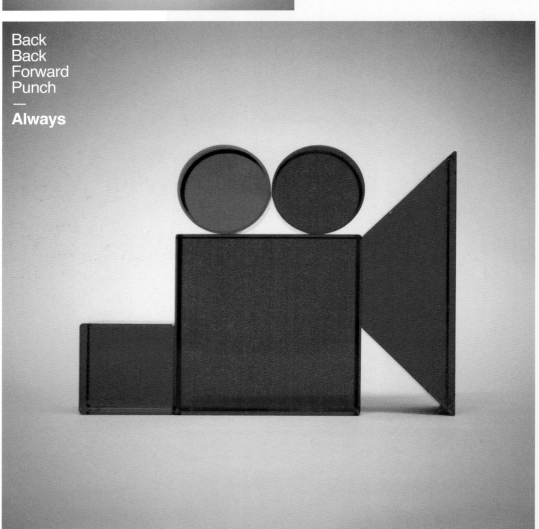

166

Always / Red Boots

Modular artwork with an intent to connect the simultaneous release of Back Back Forward Punch's electro twin set. Based on a mutual love for colour, geometry and simplicity, primary shapes and strict RGB palette created a bold, colourful and scalable graphic system applying across web and print marketing materials.

AXXONN
National Tour 2011

Axxonn National Tour

A unique iteration for electronic artist AXXONN's national tour in
Australia based on an artwork system Killen previously
developed for music initiative, New Weird Australia. Each shape
in the bespoke AXXONN geometric logotype represents a different
date of the tour, further delineated by a unique colour.

Design: Heath Killen / Client: New Weird Australia

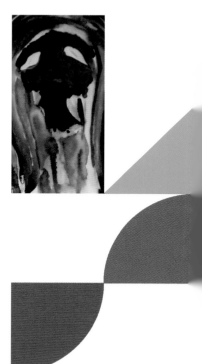

New Editions

Various covers for New Editions, New Weird Australia's record label for Australian experimental and electronic music. Expanding on the initiative's visual identity system also developed by Killen, each cover was customised based on a four-panel grid, with artworks and images supplied by individual artists or groups.

Design: Heath Killen / Client: New Weird Australia

169

Unpopular Music

Poster and accompanying album art composed for Unpopular Music,
a benefit concert for FBi Radio where New Weird Australia partook. This poster
effectively acted as the template for future designs, with a four-panel grid
filled with elements from a curated library of images,
shapes, colours and textures.

Design: Heath Killen / Client: New Weird Australia

New Weird Australia

Friday 23rd July
Red Rattler
6 Faversham Street
Marrickville
NSW

Tickets $10
Doors 7:30

Anonymeye
Erasers
Ambrose Chapel
Textile Audio
TR-10 (Lukasz Karluk & Gentleforce)

newweirdaustralia.com

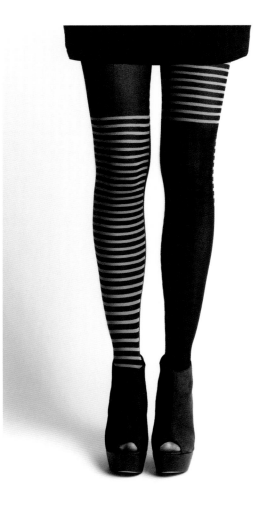

Patternity –
Fundamental Shapes Collection

Given a different theme, such as Totem and Trademark, these made-to-order
screenprinted tights display the geometric patterns that surround us everyday.
Each item is packaged and delivered in tubes with matching designs.

Design: Patternity / Packaging: Assembly / Photo: Neil Watson

Emotional Icons on Frozen Streets

Lookbook for RHLS' autumn/winter collection 2012. Looking to the future for inspirations, RHLS' creative trajectory embarks on "The Planet Z of Funness". As these fashion heros night-ski to the edge of this world, shapes meld into form, representing an oil well and later, a face.

Art Direction & Clothing: Ruffeo Hearts Lil' Snotty (RHLS) /
Illustration & Design: Ell Heuer / Photo: Jena Cumbo

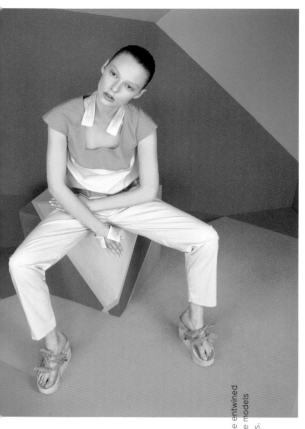

COLOR PROJECT

Far from the gloomy mood of chilly winter, this fall collection centred around the entwined effects of bold colours, proportions and asymmetry. The robotic aspect of the models bears the future fetish of futurism and the world of Bauhaus costumes.

Design: Dóri Tomcsányi / Photo: Gergo Gónczol

The shape I think about most when I am doing a composition is triangle. The accute points of a triangle create dynamism, dominance, speed and power. Although a triangle can be built with three sides of equal length, there is always movement in the shape. One angle always takes the lead while the (other) two less dominant angles have to follow. Regardless of which culture you are from and from which direction you read an image or text, triangles always have a leader angle, which just varies from person to person.

Circle holds a special fascination for me, it represents so many things but for me it makes me think of the Moon. This magical planet that holds such a sway over our planet, it is the only celestial body other than Earth on which humans have set foot. And in 1969 (the year of my birth) astronauts Neil Armstrong and Buzz Aldrin were those humans to set foot on the Moon. I often look up at the Moon and try to imagine what that must have been like, to stand there and look at Earth, truly awe inspiring. A true moment of wonder and achievement.

Carl Kleiner

Build

Back to basics — I love geometry and work with it in almost every project we do. It is like a drug you can't stop using basic shapes.

All graphic design projects can be made with a circle, a triangle and a square — it just depends on the way you use it in the concept and the way you synthesise them with the project.

If you can resume the idea using these shapes it will be (simply direct) and easy. And it will become a universal language.

Hey

I found inspiration in right triangles. They have 90° angles and a slope called a, hypotenuse. The right triangle's gift is that it is hard to tell when it is standing up or laying down. Are we looking at a little mountain from the side or a room's floor plan from above? That spatial ambiguity is a theme I like to explore in my work.

Matthew Korbel-Bowers

All shapes have an inherent, mathematical beauty - but their power, at least in design, lies in their ability to transform. Shapes are building blocks. They are mutable objects that can be dissected, reconstructed, combined. They provide surfaces that can be treated. Spaces that can be filled. They can be windows. Or grids. Containers or obstructions. Whether they are used to frame or to give form, they allow us to physically describe thought. From the simplicity of a geodesic dome - we create, understand and deconstruct our world with shapes.

Heath Killen

THE SECRET AGENT

URAUFFÜHRUNG 22.06.2010
PRINZREGENTENTHEATER

BALLETT Terrence Kohler
MUSIK Philip Glass
CHOREOGRAPHIE Terence Kohler
BÜHNE Jordi Roig
SOLISTEN UND ENSEMBLE
DES BAYERISCHEN STAATSBALLETTS

Information und Karten
www.staatsoper.de

Bayerisches
Staatsballett

Bavarian State Ballet

Several posters for various ballet performances organised by opera company, the Bavarian State Opera in Munich. Stills of dancers in each performance were played up with intersecting shapes to highlight the dynamism and spirit in individual shows.

Design: Fons Hickmann, Thomas Kronbichler, Björn Wolf (Fons Hickmann m23) / Client: Bavarian State Opera

SELLE

...UFFÜHRUNG 19.06.2010
...ZREGENTENTHEATER

...T Mats Ek
... UND KOSTÜME Marie-Louise Ekman
...N UND ENSEMBLE
...ERISCHEN STAATSBALLETTS

...und Karten: T 089 21 85 1920
...taatsballett.de

2009 SPIELZEIT 2010

PREMIEREN

VIELFÄLTIGKEIT. FORMEN VON
STILLE UND LEERE Nacho Duato 23.12.2009
ARTIFACT ... 2010
THE SECRET AGENT ... 2010
THE FORSYTHE COMPANY — YES WE CAN'T ... 25.04.2010

REPERTOIRE

100 JAHRE BALLETS RUSSES
... Bronislawa Nijinska, Terence Kohler
LE CORSAIRE Ivan Liška, Marius Petipa
GISELLE – MATS EK
DIE KAMELIENDAME John Neumeier
ONEGIN ... Cranko
RAYMONDA Marius Petipa, Ray Barra
DER STURM ...
ZUGVÖGEL ...
TERPSICHORE GALA IX UND X
BALLETTFESTWOCHEN 2010 25. April bis 9. Mai

Information und Karten: T 089 2185 ...
www.staatsballett.de

Bayerisches
Staatsballett

MASURCA FOGO

...ANZTHEATER WUPPERTAL PINA BAUSCH
...AB 28.04.2010
...ATIONALTHEATER MÜNCHEN

INSZENIERUNG UND CHOREOGRAPHIE ...
BALLETT ...
BÜHNE Peter ...
KOSTÜME ...
MUSIKALISCHE MITARBEIT ...
Andreas Eisenschneider

Information und Karten: ... 1920
www.staatsballett.de

Bayerisches
Staatsballett

Daily Poetry

Daily Poetry is an imaginary exhibition, introducing the work of three American photographers, who were at the forefront of colour photography in the 1970s. Fragments of their work were highlighted in the posters with hints of the epoch.

Design: Clara Fernández

RY
—

Short

09.10.10 /
18 hs

46 fotografías de stephen Short,
conocido por sus inexpresivas imáge-
nes, escenas banales,paisajes rurales,
calles, pueblos y objetos típicos
de los Estados Unidos.

C11-69-AD, Buenos.Todo el espacio de Fundación cuenta .

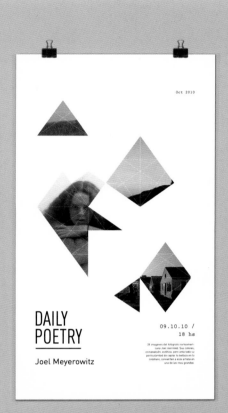

Oct 2010

DAILY
POETRY

Joel Meyerowitz

09.10.10 /
18 hs

38 imagenes del fotógrafo norteameri-
cano Joel Sternfeld. Sus colores,
composición, estética, pero una todo su
particularidad de captar la belleza en lo
cotidiano, convierten a este artista en
uno de los mas grandes

Oct 2010

DAILY
POETRY

Joel Sternfeld

09.10.10 /
18 hs

38 fotografías de Joel Sternfeld que
encuentran elementos enigmáticos y
extraños , una suplmento, un gesto,
una mirada, una disparación en el
espacio o una curiosidad efímera

NEWCASTLE FESTIVAL OF DANCE

JULY 2010

www.nfd.co.uk

Newcastle Festival of Dance

Posters publicising the Newcastle Festival of Dance as a festival for everyone.
Shoes designed for various dance on the feet of different generations call on kids to learn,
teens to be creative and the elderly to recollect their time spent in the old ballrooms.

Design: Amy Rodchester

NEWCASTLE FESTIVAL OF DANCE

JULY 2010

•••

www.nfd.co.uk

NEWCASTLE FESTIVAL OF DANCE

JULY 2010

•••

www.nfd.co.uk

NEWCASTLE FESTIVAL OF DANCE

JULY 2010

•••

www.nfd.co.uk

B-Side

Event identity for the second edition of B-Side, a modernistic jewellery festival with exhibitions and performances held across Amsterdam. Geometric imagery were used to dress up classic jewellery in its most playful yet coherent sense.

Design: Holy Grey / Client: B-Side

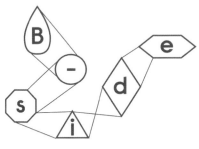

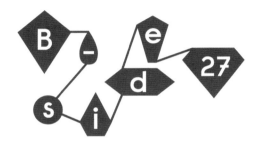

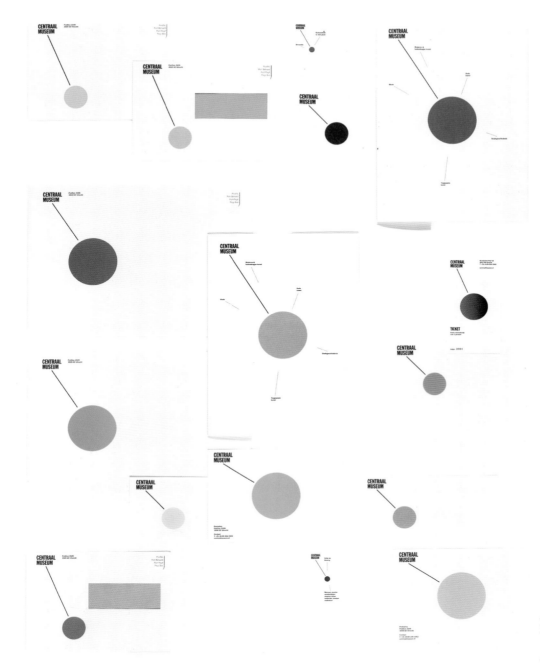

Centraal Museum

Catching people's eye with its position, size and colours, the big round dot represents
Centraal Museum's central location in the Netherlands and its role as Utrecht's cultural hub.
The circle extends to guide visitors' way inside the building.

Design: Lesley Moore / Client: Centraal Museum / Photo: Vincent Zedelius

EXPO 6

AUDITORIUM

EXPO 10

10.1 sat –12.25 sun,
2011

LabACT vol.01
The EyeWriter

視線を通じて世界と繋がる。
「視線入力技術」

The EyeWriter（ジ・アイライター）
Zach Lieberman, Evan Roth, James Powderly, Theo Watson, Chris Sugrue, TEMPT1
エキソニモ
セミトラ

山口情報芸術センター【YCAM】
http://labact.ycam.jp/

12.4 sun –3.25 sun,
2012

LabACT vol.02
Eye-Tracking Informatics

視線を通じて世界と繋がる。
「視線入力技術」

三上晴子
アイトラッキング・インフォマティクス
「Eye-Tracking Informatics～視線のモルフォロジー」

山口情報芸術センター【YCAM】
http://labact.ycam.jp/

194

LabACT Series Exhibition vol.01 & vol.02

Exhibition graphics for *LabACT*, an exhibition on creative and social values through a dialogue between science and art. "The EyeWriter" and "Eye-tracking Technology" were part of the research. A typeface with zigzag lines symbolise eye movements, whereas circles and crosses illustrate focal points.

Design: Studiokanna / Client: The Yamaguchi Center for Arts and Media (YCAM)

LabACTの目ざすもの

メディア技術と社会の関わりを、

本質的には人間存在と人間科学のあり

より身近な用途や近い未来の必然性

して術が多くの人

理由がさまざまな目に見えない

新しい技術が、いまここに生まれるこ

Tokyo Polytechnic University

Made of two campuses, Tokyo Polytechnic University, a.k.a. Tokyo KOGEI University, is a private university offering education in both the fields of arts and technology. A bold and sleek logo symbolic of duality was first installed to refresh the institute's image in 2005, followed by signage systems completed in 2012.

Design: Hiromura Design Office / Client: Tokyo Polytechnic University / Photo: Yasuo Kondo, Nacása & Partners

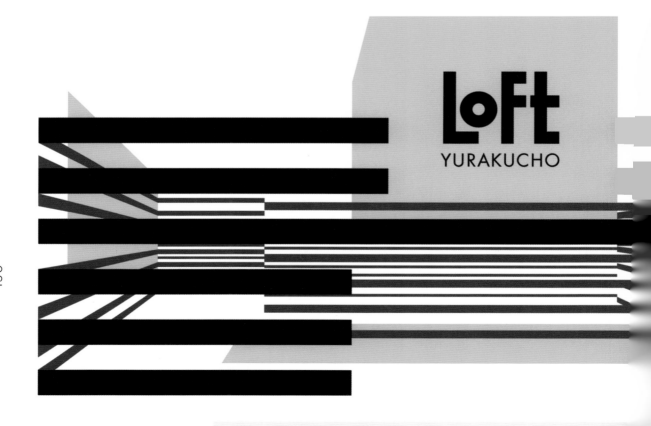

YURAKUCHO LOFT

Poster campaign and corresponding accessories celebrating Loft's new branch grand opening. While the site is still empty, the campaign offers the public a sneak peak of the to-be very roomy shopping space with transparent walls and 3D layout. The message stands out in Japanese chain store's bright corporate colours, yellow and black.

Design: Hiromura Design Office / Client: THE LOFT Co., Ltd. / Interior & Photo: Tonerico

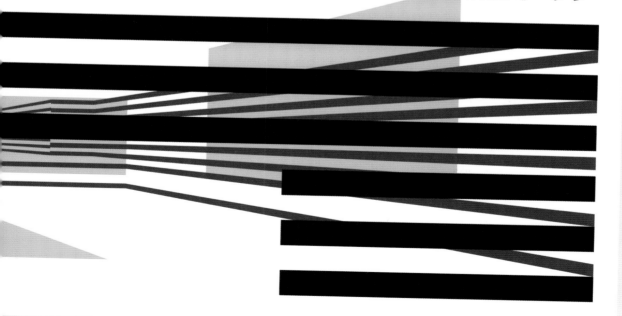

LOFT YURAKUCHO
9.1 [THU] OPEN
有楽町ロフト 9月1日 [木] 有楽町 インフォス1F オープン

LOFT
YURAKUCHO
2011.9.1
[THU]
NEW OPEN

YURAKU

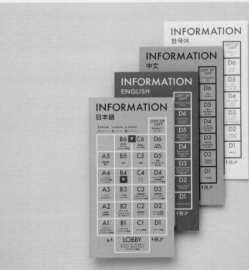

LOFT YURAKUCHO 9.1 [THU] OPEN
有楽町ロフト 9月1日［木］有楽町 インフォス1F オープン

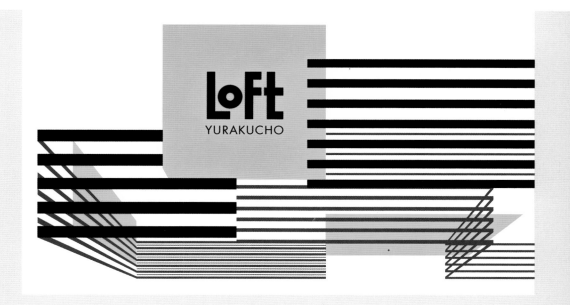

LOFT YURAKUCHO 9.1 [THU] OPEN
有楽町ロフト 9月1日［木］有楽町 インフォス1F オープン

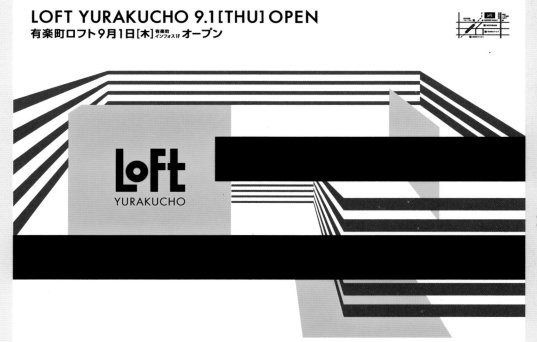

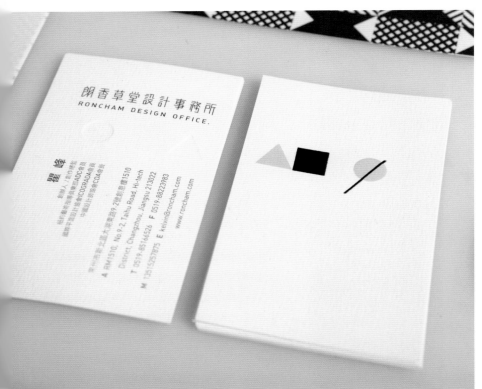

Roncham Design Identity

The presence of squares and circles in Roncham's identity has its origin in the philosophic concept of "yin and yang", indicating "branding" as a fusion of technics and art. The concept recurs assertively on Roncham's collateral as a march, from "outstanding" to "excellence".

Design: Kelvin Qu

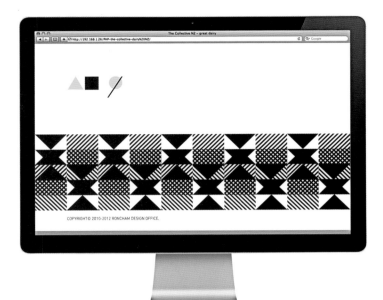

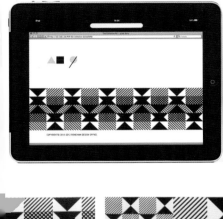

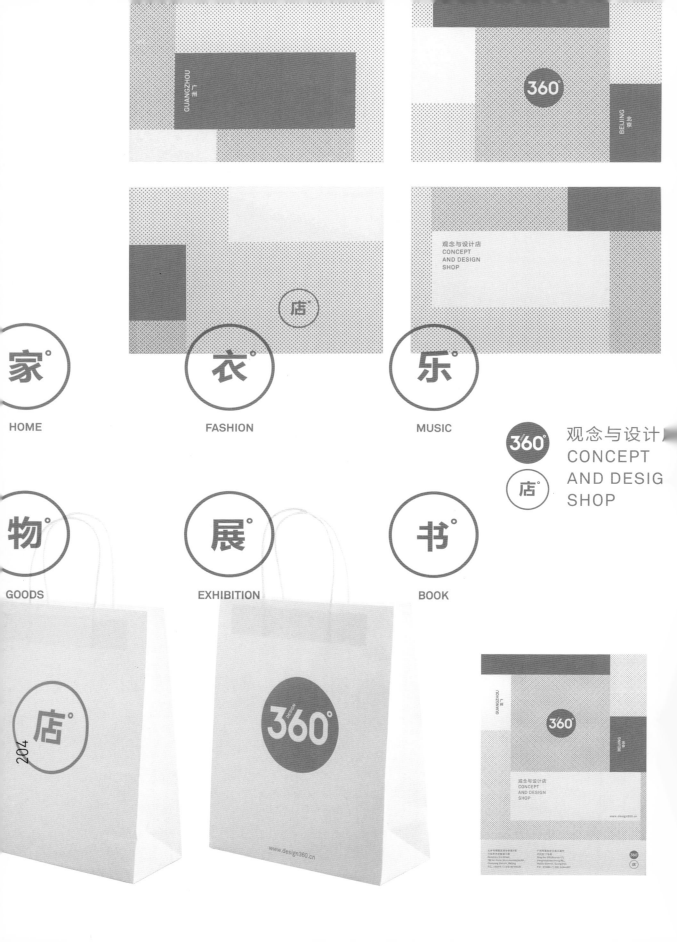

GUANGZHOU 广州

360°

BEIJING 北京

观念与设计店
CONCEPT
AND DESIGN
SHOP

家° | HOME
衣° | FASHION
乐° | MUSIC
店°
物° | GOODS
展° | EXHIBITION
书° | BOOK

360° 观念与设计店
CONCEPT
店° AND DESIG
SHOP

店°

360°

204

www.design360.cn

360° Shop

Identity and signage for the new concept store and showroom at Beijing's 798 Art Zone, with visual connections to its root in magazine, Design 360°. The fluorescent red stands for contemporary China and the new Asian creative force behind.

Design: Milkxhake / Client: Sandu Publishing Co., Ltd

观念与设计店
CONCEPT
AND DESIGN
SHOP

北京市朝阳区酒仙桥路4号
798艺术区陶瓷三街
Ceramics 3rd Street,
798 Art Zone,
No.4 Jiuxianqiao Rd.,
Chaoyang District, Beijing
P.C. :100015 / T: 010-59789476

广州市海珠区江南大道中
255号17号店
Shop No.255 (Branch 17),
Jiangnandadaozhong Rd.,
Haizhu District, Guangzhou
P.C. :510280 / T: 020-34344887

www.design360.cn

BEIJING
GUANGZHOU 北京 广州

向东方
店 长
M:15989200992

北京市朝阳区酒仙桥路4号
798艺术区陶瓷三街
Ceramics 3rd Street,
798 Art Zone, No.4 Jiuxianqiao Rd.,
Chaoyang District, Beijing
P.C. :100015 / T: 010-59789476
F: 010-57623060

广州市海珠区江南大道中255号17号店
Shop No.255 (Branch 17),
Jiangnandaozhong Rd.,
Haizhu District, Guangzhou
P.C. :510280 / T: 020-34344887

www.design360.cn
360shop.gz@gmail.com

Run Run Shaw Creative Media Centre Grand Opening

Crafted by Daniel Libeskind, the new Creative Media Centre marks a new era for creativity and professional training in the scene. The diagonal lines in the school's identity deliver the quality of 'substance' and 'details' in the architecture's spirit and iconic form.

Design: Milkxhake / Client: City University of Hong Kong / Photo: John Gollings

RUN RUN SHAW
CREATIVE
MEDIA CENTRE
GRAND OPENING
AND FESTIVAL

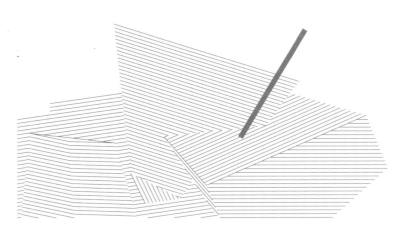

ABOUT
RUN RUN SHAW
CREATIVE MEDIA
CENTRE

A landmark design by the renowned architect Daniel Libeskind,
the Run Run Shaw Creative Media Centre is one of the most advanced
teaching and research facilities in the world. Its superbly equipped and
inspiring environment is an international meeting point for creative media
professionals, and a hotbed where student-staff interaction,
interdisciplinary collaboration and synergies with industry can flourish.
Exploring the integration of cutting edge techniques, technologies and
ideas, this iconic centre sets a new Asian benchmark for digital media
education and artistic innovation at home and abroad.

MOBILE
進行
YAU MA TEI 油麻地
15.5-10.6.2012

Mobile M+: Yau Ma Tei

Being the first of the art exhibitions series, *M+* brought in six sizable installations on the streets to challenge the layered narratives of Hong Kong. Where positive and negative forms referred to the ties between artists and the community, simple forms contrasted the old and crowded district with a contemporary touch.

Nam Pak Cultural Day

Nam Pak Cultural Day was a venue where traditional craftsmanship from southern and northern China meet. With a strong sense of joyous communion, the equally-bold yet distinctive blue and red come in perfect circles to reflect the energy as the opposite cultures intersect.

Design: TGIF / Client: The Conservancy Association Centre for Heritage

Cornwall Design Season

Branding and collateral for Cornwall Design Season, a festival of original thinking, making and doing. Where 16 "design stories" would be exhibited in 16 shipping containers based on the story's theme, the equal number of symbols with robust contents were devised. Humble or astonishing, they represent the changes these stories bring.

Design: A-Side Studio / Client: Dott / Festival creative direction: Peter Kirby

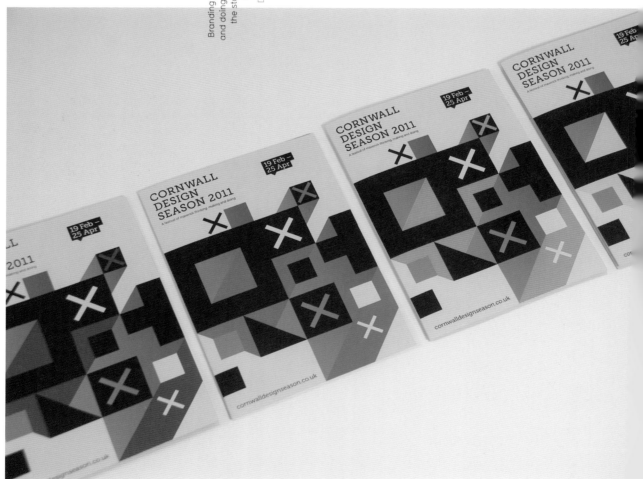

 CORNWALL
DESIGN
SEASON 2011

 CORNWALL
DESIGN
SEASON 2011

 CORNWALL
DESIGN
SEASON 2011

 CORNWALL
DESIGN
SEASON 2011

 CORNWALL
DESIGN
SEASON 2011

 CORNWALL
DESIGN
SEASON 2011

Brasília 50 anos

Brasília 50 anos

50 Years Brasília Anniversary

Promotional graphics celebrating 50 years of Brasília since it became the national capital for Brazil. Taking one of Brasília's landmark, the Palácio do Congresso Nacional, as a starting point, the outline of the building was reduced to its essence assembling the number '50'.

Design: Rejane Dal Bello / Client: City of Brasília

Brasília 50 anos

Brasília 50 anos

Kieler Woche #3

Identity aspired to excite the city of Kiel during Kieler Woche 2011, the world's largest sailing event. Random letter codes adopted from the international maritime flag language was

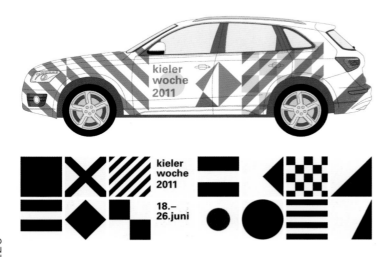

AG2R LA MONDIALE
TRANSAT
L'UNIQUE TRANSAT EN
DOUBLE À ARMES ÉGALES
10E ÉDITION, CONCARNEAU SAINT-BARTH
DÉPART DIMANCHE 18 AVRIL 2010
WWW.TRANSAT.AG2RLAMONDIALE.FR

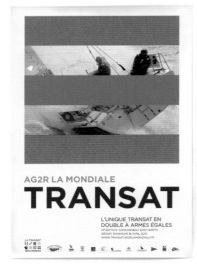

AG2R LA MONDIALE
TRANSAT
L'UNIQUE TRANSAT EN
DOUBLE À ARMES ÉGALES
10E ÉDITION, CONCARNEAU SAINT-BARTH
DÉPART DIMANCHE 18 AVRIL 2010
WWW.TRANSAT.AG2RLAMONDIALE.FR

AG2R LA MONDIALE
TRANSAT
L'UNIQUE TRANSAT EN
DOUBLE À ARMES ÉGALES
10E ÉDITION, CONCARNEAU SAINT-BARTH
DÉPART DIMANCHE 18 AVRIL 2010
WWW.TRANSAT.AG2RLAMONDIALE.FR

LA TRANSAT
AG2R LA MONDIALE

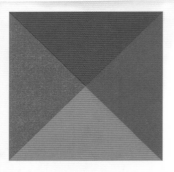

AG2R LA MONDIALE
TRANSAT
L'UNIQUE TRANSAT EN
DOUBLE À ARMES ÉGALES
10E ÉDITION, CONCARNEAU SAINT-BARTH
DÉPART DIMANCHE 18 AVRIL 2010
WWW.TRANSAT.AG2RLAMONDIALE.FR

AG2R LA MONDIALE
TRANSAT
L'UNIQUE TRANSAT EN
DOUBLE À ARMES ÉGALES
10E ÉDITION, CONCARNEAU SAINT-BARTH
DÉPART DIMANCHE 18 AVRIL 2010
WWW.TRANSAT.AG2RLAMONDIALE.FR

AG2R LA MONDIALE
TRANSAT
L'UNIQUE TRANSAT EN
DOUBLE À ARMES ÉGALES
10E ÉDITION, CONCARNEAU SAINT-BARTH
DÉPART DIMANCHE 18 AVRIL 2010
WWW.TRANSAT.AG2RLAMONDIALE.FR

Ag2r La Mondiale – La Transat

La Transat is an international yacht race sponsored by Ag2r La Mondiale. Water sports and the sponsor were linked with scintillating colours and shapes referencing client's house colours and the international maritime flag signals.

Design: Rejane Dal Bello (Studio Dumbar), Danny Kreeft / Client: Ag2r La Mondiale

State of Design Festival Identity

To embody the festival's theme of Design That Moves, the event hinged on simple shapes to bond all demographic and design disciplines. The shapes were explored as heaving fluids to imply how simple things become complex and vice versa in design.

Design: SouthsouthWest / Client: State of Design Festival (Victorian State Government Australia) / Photo: Tobiaz Titz, Adam Gibson (SouthsouthWest)

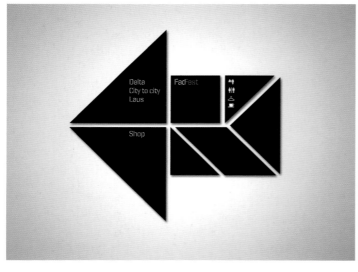

FadFest

FadFest is a week-long celebration jointly organised by FAD's seven design association members in Spain. As well as the content, the tangram paradox imparts imagination, problem-solving and spatial intelligence at the heart of the event.

Design: Studio Astrid Stavro, Grafica / Client: Foster in Arts & Design

CRYSTALS & LASERS

Aerosol mural celebrating the opening of MWM's solo exhibition, *Crystals & Lasers*, composed during his one-month stay in Paris. Recognised as his "Vectorfunk" style, his work explored his dedication to various art disciplines and the vibrancy of Paris.

Design: MWM Graphics

Vincci Bit Hotel @ Barcelona

Mega mural creating a dazzling colour story along the 50-meter long corridor on the fourth floor of Vincci Bit Hotel, Barcelona. The ratios of colour consistently change as guests walk through the aisle, from one end to the other.

Design: MWM Graphics / Curation: Beriestain Interiores

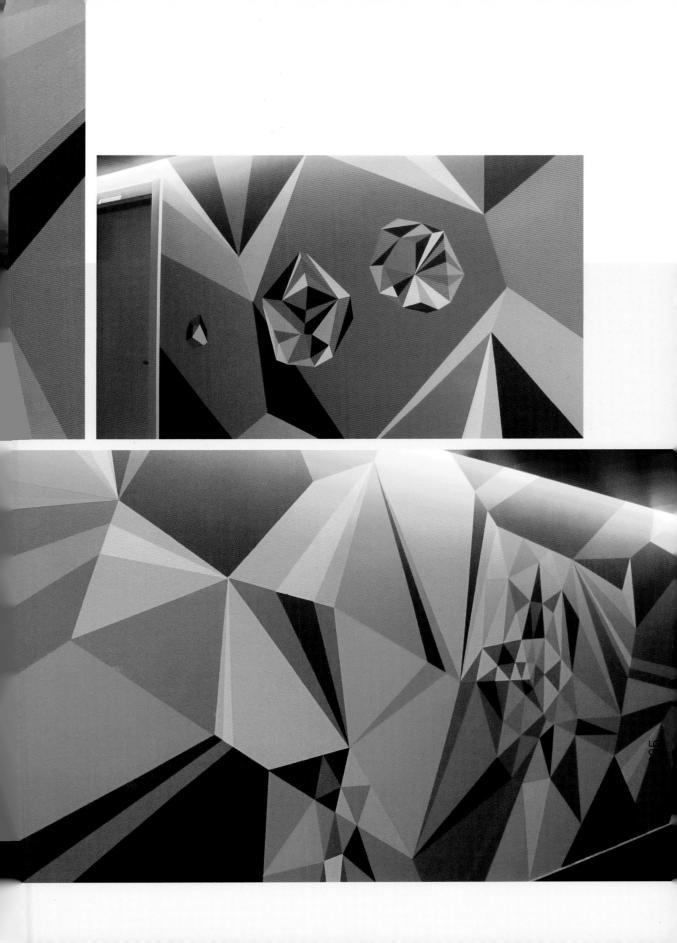

Dream Maker

A miniature solar system tied to visitors' fortune and dreams at the lobby of the Indianapolis Museum of Art in the States. Filled with air and dangling in vibrant colours, these buddies' job was to bring good luck to visitors upon their entrance.

Design: FriendsWithYou

Rainbow City

Coming in a vibrant array of rainbow colours, 40 interactive inflatable mushrooms, balloons and lollies were installed to sweep the New York City and High Line Park's new section two with colours and joy.
The happy city was on site for almost a month to lure visitors into exploring the giant playground in 2011.

Design: FriendsWithYou

ON THE MOVE

Geometric graphics are not exclusive to print work. After the mute and still, it's time for some music, stories and motion pictures!

Get your smartphone and QR code reader ready to watch some clips! This section showcases how creatives draw on the simple forms of shapes to model characters, narrate and visualise music contents in 28 multimedia projects, including music videos, promos, call-ups, short animations and screen introductions.

AICP
STUDIO AKA, Blacklist

Alligator Pop
Benjamin Ang

ANACONDA
Iain Acton

City Planning
ONIONSKIN

Coldplay
Universal Everything

Composition in Red
Tendril Design + Animation

Conductor
Alexander Chen

Hululu Honglonglong Hualala
Lei Lei

Human Orchestra
Takashi Ohashi

Interac Flash Tutorial
Tendril Design + Animation

Kraddy — Android Porn
MUSCLEBEAVER

Le Vilain Petit Carré
Charles Klipfel & Quentin Carnicelli

MTV Hits
Universal Everything

My...My...
Lei Lei

Only The Brave Foundation
Brand New School

Pausefest Melbourne — Director's Cut
Sander van Dijk

Resonance: The Interpreter's House
Jorge R. Canedo Estrada

Science Museum — Who Am I?
STUDIO AKA

Sonar
Renaud Hallée

The Camera Collection
Antonio Vicentini

The GRID
Tomas Markevičius

The Seed
Johnny Kelly

To Do List
Tendril Design + Animation

Toob — Wavaphon
Mr Kaplin

transmediale.11
Büro Achter April

Weather Tests
Savas Ozay

Where Things Come From
Design Bureau :: Hardy Seiler

Yeah Just There
STUDIO AKA

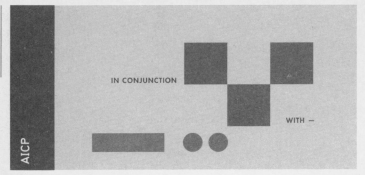

AICP

As the opener of the prestigious 2012 AICP Awards show held at MoMA, AKA devised a sequence wherein shapes drift hypnotically against a tailored soundscape by Antfood, in hands with the AICP team. As well as end credits, the visual elements were also applied as the 23 category ident spots in the show.

STUDIO AKA, Blacklist

Direction: Christopher Gray (STUDIO AKA)
Production: STUDIO AKA, Blacklist
Music: Antfood
Client: AICP New York

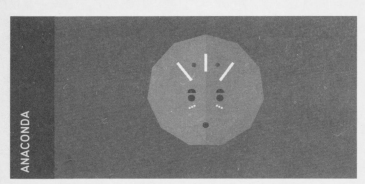

Alligator Pop

Started off as a rendering of Singapore's local art scene for Baybeats Festival 2011, this short clip takes viewers to trip through a creative world filled with avidity and surprises. Together with Ang's own audio track, each sound note was interpreted and translated into visuals, representing the general whole.

Benjamin Ang

Design/Production: Benjamin Ang
Client: Baybeats Singapore 2011

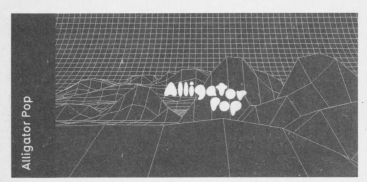

ANACONDA

Contrary to horrible screams one can relate to the giant snake, Anaconda explores synchronisation of images and sound based on a namesake dubstep track by British artist, Untold. Syncopated rhythms illuminate in the interchange of animated patterns and characters with brief movements and cheer.

Iain Acton

Design/Production: Iain Acton
Music: Untold

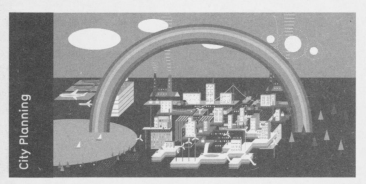

City Planning

City Planning is a vivid rendition of a namesake track by alternative rock band, Doit Science. Imagining Tokyo's rise, the video observes the city starting up as a flat hamlet from a fixed point and later, on the move as it expands. The city's growth is also illustrated with an extra dimension as it turns into a metropolis.

ONIONSKIN

Design/Production: ONIONSKIN
Music: Doit Science

Coldplay

Dubbed "Fuzzyman" because he morphs persistently, striding, running and flying in neon thorns, pixels, tubes and laser beams along with Coldplay's music. Fuzzyman was modelled as the mascot of the band's ongoing world tour and the opening and closing visuals of their headline show at Glastonbury 2011.

Universal Everything

Creative Direction/Animation:
Universal Everything
Character: Paul Clayton
Client: Coldplay

Composition in Red

Deconstruction and reconstruction are constantly at the heart of Tendril's creative trajectory. The sound-synchronised sequence puts on view how their logo was conceived from a lunchbox of minimal geometric elements. Graphic elements were also drawn from their recent projects as the backbone of the edit.

Tendril Design + Animation

Design/Production:
Tendril Design + Animation

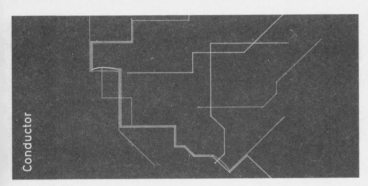

Conductor

Mute at the beginning until the lines crisscross, Conductor turns New York's subway system into an acoustic string instrument. The piece begins in real time as the MTA trains spawn in reality and continues to accelerate in a 24-hour loop. The visuals are based on Massimo Vignelli's diagram designed in 1972.

Alexander Chen

Design/Production: Alexander Chen
Music: Corsica_S

Hululu Honglonglong Hualala

One day, a rain storm arrived and broke the peace of a village. Wind started blowing hats off and lightening struck the ground, but the villagers found their way to enjoy the mess until the flood came and flushed a kid out into the universe. The title is the onomatopoeic expression for thunders.

Lei Lei

Animation: Lei Lei
Music: Li Xingyu

Human Orchestra

Human Orchestra presents an impressionistic view of classic city space with flashes and sounds typical of any megacity around the world. Capitalising on a dynamic switch of space, the clip offers viewers a cinematographic experience with minimal graphics and matching sounds.

Takashi Ohashi

Direction/Animation: Takashi Ohashi
Music: Yoshito Onishi

Interac Flash Tutorial

An information-rich tutorial featuring a lipsync wallet character, encouraging shoppers to opt for Interac debit card. For a better impact, visuals were kept minimal and graphic with the pace maintained by unexpected twists, snappy animation timing and swift transitions.

Tendril Design + Animation

Agency: Agency59
Design: Tendril Design + Animation,
Chico Jofilsan, Daniel Pommella, Cristiane Ly
Production: Tendril Design + Animation,
Chico Jofilsan, Daniel Pommella
Client: Interac

Kraddy — Android Porn

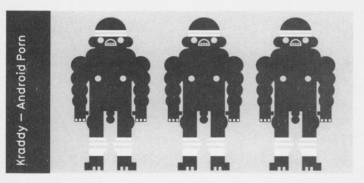

In Kraddy's track, the theme of sex is explicit. So for its video, MUSCLEBEAVER takes it the implicit way, by comparing the rhythmical movements in lovemaking to bodybuilding and playing up its sense of power and violence. Black and white were particularly adopted to cohere with EQX Records' unique identity.

MUSCLEBEAVER

Design/production: MUSCLEBEAVER
Music: Kraddy (Original), Mochipet (Remix)
Client: Equinox Records

Le Vilain Petit Carré (The Ugly Square)

What would the world be like if it's all made of squares? And if one day a circle turns up, would it be able to fit in? Stimulated by the classic *The Ugly Duckling*, the circle becomes "the ugly square" in the world of square. It might be a lonely circle at first, but its adventure is yet another beautiful story to learn about.

Charles Klipfel & Quentin Carnicelli

Design/Production:
Charles Klipfel & Quentin Carnicelli
Music: Neal Williams

MTV Hits

A series of promos created to rebrand the MTV channel worldwide, stressing and celebrating MTV as pop culture and thus the ethos 'Pop x 1000%'. The project deals with a vast range of pop music genre, including pop, electro, boy bands and hip hop.

Universal Everything

Creative Direction:
MTV WDS, Universal Everything
Concept/Direction/Animation:
Universal Everything
Audio: Wevie.tv
Client: MTV WDS

My...My...

Part fantasy, part reality, My...My... tells a curious incidence of a guy who found himself naked in a mysterious landscape and experienced a rough journey as he tried to retrieve his clothes. Like a silent film, there were no spoken dialogues. The clip is complimented with intertitles and video game tracks.

Lei Lei

Animation: Lei Lei
Music: Li Xingyu

Only The Brave Foundation

A two-and-a half minute call-to-arms for Only The Brave Foundation, produced to inspire and mobilise the youth to join forces and help end extreme poverty in Africa and around the globe. BNS has suggested a unique storytelling approach fashioned to look like being played using a handcranked projector.

Brand New School

Creative Agency: Antidote
Direction: Jonathan Notaro
Production: Brand New School
Music/Audio: Human Worldwide
Client: Only the Brave Foundation

Pausefest Melbourne – Director's Cut

"Reach out", "share", "demonstrate" are how artists get better at what they love to do. With 99 percent of the animation vector which continues to racterise, the clip communicates the concept of Pause Fest 2011 in a very abstract way. A tutorial clip is also produced to share van Dijk's insights on colour approach.

Sander van Dijk

Concept/Motion Design: Sander van Dijk
Music/Audio:
Dane Middleton (Brightling Sound)
Voice-over: Jaclyn Blumas

Resonance: The Interpreter's House

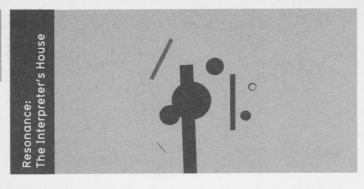

An abstract animation with mixed emotions developed based on a section of John Bunyan's *The Pilgrim's Progress* (1678), where Christian is guided through the Interpreter's House. Nevertheless, emphases were placed on giving meaning to animations rather than relating the story with graphics and sounds.

Jorge R. Canedo Estrada

Design/Production:
Jorge R. Canedo Estrada
Audio: David Kamp
Client: Simon Jones, SR Partners

Science Museum – Who Am I?

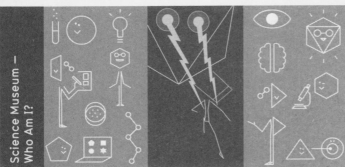

An one-minute animated screen introduction for *Who Am I?*, an exhibition at the Science Museum where visitors can explore their identity by experiencing "science in action". Extracting mathematical precision from science, an abstracted scientist was created to provoke visitors' curiosity at the site.

STUDIO AKA

Direction/Design:
Grant Orchard (STUDIO AKA)
Production: STUDIO AKA
Audio: Nic Gill
Client: The Science Museum, London

Sonar

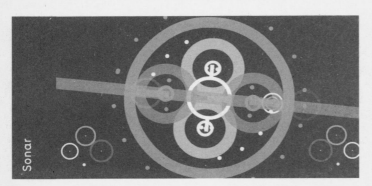

Sonar visualises the conversion of sounds in sync with images in its own logic and language, basically with dots and circles indicating notes, shooting lines and numbers for their duration and colours to separate pitches and basses. The soundscape is progressively complex towards the middle and calms at the end.

Renaud Hallée

Design/Production: Renaud Hallée

The Camera Collection

In 2011, American designer Bill Brown created a collection of 100 pixelated cameras and accessories for public sharing and use. Based on Brown's camera illustrations, from traditional film cameras to digital SLR, Vicentini exhibits the evolution of cameras animated with structural analysis, music and colours.

Antonio Vicentini

Animation: Antonio Vicentini
Illustration: Bill Brow
Music: Ben Hantoot

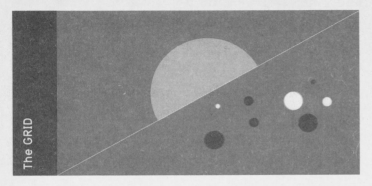

The GRID

Inspired by geometric designs and the idea that all shapes can interact in motion, the GRID started as a series of motion tests and ended as one bigger motion graphic project. Entirely animated by hand without recourse to 3D software, the clip evokes an organic unity of shapes matched with guitar sounds.

Tomas Markevičius

Design/Production: Tomas Markevičius
Music: Alphabets Heaven

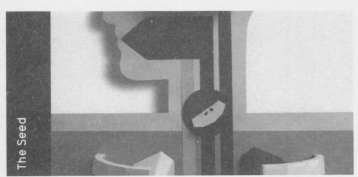

The Seed

The Seed is an epic journey of life cycle chronicled through the trials and tribulations of a humble apple seed. Combining stop-motion created with 3D papercrafts and animation made with line drawings, the ordinary life of a seed was stretched with humour and interesting details.

Johnny Kelly

Creative Direction: Keith Anderson,
Tony Stern, Frank Aldorf
Direction/Concept: Johnny Kelly
Paper Modelling: Elin Svensson
Music: Jape
Client: Adobe

To Do List

The title of this clip is self-explanatory. To Do List is a simple and sweet personal project outlining what Daniel Luna, Director of Tendril and friend Yaniv Fridman cherish and aspire to do (or not) to live their life to the full. Each of the goals is presented in both textual and graphical way.

Tendril Design + Animation

Design: Tendril Design + Animation,
Yaniv Fridman
Production: Tendril Design + Animation
Music/Audio: WhiteNoise Lab

Toob — Wavaphon

Wavaphon MV is a tribute to the old VJ graphics used to appear in techno gigs and explores mathematics in motion in line with music and rhythms. Mathematical relations were portrayed with a diversity of physics applets, which guide the overall movements and graphical approach of the piece.

Mr Kaplin

Design/Production: Mr Kaplin
Music: Toob, Process Recordings

transmediale.11

Inspired by intuitive interaction, Büro Achter April translated the concept of "Response:Ability" behind media art festival, transmediale.11, into moving images based on the event's identity devised by +Ruddigkeit. The strokes and dots resemble the units of binary system and DNA, the root of infinity.

Büro Achter April

Organisor: +Ruddigkeit
Design/Production: Büro Achter April
Client: transmediale,
Kulturprojekte Berlin GmbH
Special Credits: WALL AG

Weather Tests

Weather Tests is Ozay's exploratory project, attempting to exaggerate actions and physics of each season, with real life dynamics and personal emotions attached to them. That involves romantic snow, melancholic rain, cheerful sun and mournful winds captured like documentary shorts with vocal remarks.

Savas Ozay

Design/Production: Savas Ozay

Where Things Come From

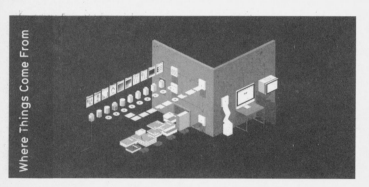

Do we still want to know where things exactly come from? Using a sequence of graphic renderings and a man's voice to narrate how we conceive knowledge in the past and now, the two-minute trailer poses a question and excites the audience's hunger to learn through different channels.

Design Bureau :: Hardy Seiler

Design/Production: Hardy Seiler
Motion Design:
Jascha Müller, Jonathan Winkler
Audio: Torsten Strer
Text: Hardy Seiler, Daniel Nauck
Voice-over: Peter Bennett

Yeah Just There

By visual festival boffin, ONEDOTZERO's invitation, AKA created an array of sound-based graphics for graphic wallpaper creator, Granimator, on the theme of erotic pleasure. On ONEDOTZERO's 15th birthday, the elements were sequenced as a "love letter" with a nod to the British digital arts group's work.

STUDIO AKA

Direction/Design:
Grant Orchard (STUDIO AKA)
Production: STUDIO AKA
Sound: Nic Gill
Client: ONEDOTZERO, USTWO

Acton, Iain

Action is a British animator and illustrator.
P. 242

Ang, Benjamin

Born in 1991 and raised in Singapore, the motion designer graduated in Motion Graphics & Broadcast Design at Nanyang Polytechnic. He loves to experiment with different styles of design and let his imagination take over while listening to music. He is constantly looking to enrich his experience in the industry and try out new techniques and ideas.
P. 242

ARTIVA DESIGN

A creative studio located in Genoa, Italy, since 2003. Its work is based on the interest of two designers, Daniele De Batté and Davide Sossi, in visual art, graphics, illustration and multimedia.
P. 110-111, 115

Artworklove

Composed of Caroline de Vries, Marion Laurens and Ben Reece who founded the studio in 2009, Artworklove creates original identities, prints and digital materials for clients in the fields of arts and culture, luxury, moving image and publishing in Paris.
P. 013

A-Side Studio

A-Side studio creates and nurtures successful brands by providing art directions, graphic design and illustration while jumping freely between image and product, design and art, flat pages and motion pictures.
P. 045, 214-217

Atipus

Barcelona-based graphic communication studio, specialising in corporate identity, art direction, packaging, editorial and web services. Atipus has been continually awarded by national and European design honours, e.g. Laus Awards, ADC*E Awards, Anuaria.
P. 122

Bello, Rejane Dal

Currently a senior graphic designer and illustrator at Studio Dumbar, Bello joined them during her Master study at Post St. Joost Academy. Originally from Rio de Janeiro, Bello is based in the Netherlands since 2004. She is now also a teacher at where she took the master degree.
P. 080-083, 218-219, 222-223

BERG

Working seamlessly across media including prints, screen and the environment, BERG is an independent ideas studio based in the UK. It has an international reputation for innovation, imagination and sound commercial values working closely with clients and industry professionals to create solutions that are considered, engaging and effective.
P. 072-073

BLOW

Established in 2010 by Ken Lo, who graduated from HKU SPACE Community College in visual communication and won the champion of "Design Student of The Year", BLOW specialises in brand identity, publications, environmental graphics, web site design, etc..
P. 034-035

Bowers, Matthew Korbel

An artist and designer from Northern California, Bowers spends his days working at a global branding agency and his evenings making art at home. His work is beholden to water, sun, form, color, succulent plants, architecture, maps and his wife's writing.
P. 029

Brand New School

With offices in New York and Los Angeles, the vertically integrated production company and design studio delivers media on all platforms by offering a new model for creative digital production. They are filmmakers, developers, designers, animators, editors, illustrators, and producers dedicated to driving communications to new heights.
P. 245

Build

Founded in 2001, the London-based graphic design consultancy focuses on design, art direction and identity with a specialty in high-end prints. Both Build, as a studio, and Michael C. Place as a solo artist, have shown works in several exhibitions in the UK and abroad, including Tokyo, Paris, New York and London.
P. 092-097

Büro Achter April

The team works to generate disorder. By dismantling expectations, they hope to achieve a new path, a different perspective, or an unexpected breakthrough. Moving content and bringing meaning into spaces are the overall design objectives.
P. 248

Carreras, Genís

A London-based graphic designer born in Catalonia in 1987.
P. 144-145

Château-vacant

Consisting of French-born Lémuel (b. 1986), Yannick (b. 1985) and Baptiste (b. 1984), the studio was founded in 2010 in Montréal. They create images and videos, as well as illustration, photography and graphic design.
P. 030

Chen, Alexander

Based in Brooklyn, Chen (b. 1981) creates musical and interactive work, including Sonata (2002) which generated music from video footage of Philadelphia subway commuters, and ww.mta.me (2011). After working with companies such as The Barbarian Group, he

...oined Google Creative Lab in 2010, where he conceived the Les Paul Google doodle. Chen s a multiinstrumentalist who performs live on viola under musical monikers The Consulate General and Boy in Static.

P. 243

Cina Associates

Creative studio that brings great things to life.

P. 108

Cina, Michael

Internationally recognised creative director who is currently leading a multidisciplinary design studio, Cina Associates. Michael is known globally for originating graphic design boutique, YouWorkForThem, and its sister company, WeWorkForThem. His design portfolio includes many prominent Fortune 500 companies including Apple, American Express, ESPN, Pepsi, Coke, Hewlett Packard, Microsoft, Mazda, and Victoria's Secret. Michael Cina is a member of the Initiative Artist Collective.

P. 121

Clara von Zweigbergk Design

Born in Stockholm and studied at Beckmans Design School, Stockholm and Art Center College of Design, Pasadena, USA, Zweigbergk has worked as a graphic designer since 1995 and ran the multidisciplinary design studio Rivieran, with two partners in Stockholm between 1997 and 2002. After four years as a senior graphic designer at Lissoni Associati in Milan, she started her own studio in Stockholm, specialising in art directions, corporate identities, packaging and book design and a growing series of products for HAY and Artecnica.

P. 029

Couceiro , Cristiana

Born in Portugal, Couceiro studied advertising and worked as a copywriter to finally understand that she had to express herself visually. She went back to college and is now working as a designer and illustrator in Lisbon.

P. 164-165

Cundall, William

Currently a graphic design undergrad at De Montfort University, Leicester. Apart from using digital software programs, Cundall likes to experiment designs with different materials such as paint and ink. His main fascination is with different typography, compositions and colours to see if it communicates the design in a different way.

P. 086-087

Dalton, Duane

Born in Dublin, Ireland, Dalton has recently completed a Bachelor of Honors Degree in Visual Arts Practice (Fine Art) at IADT Dublin and continues to studying visual communication.

P. 112-113

Design Bureau :: Hardy Seiler

Specialising in corporate, editorial, graphic and web design, Seiler creates straightforward and compelling communication design and often collaborates with experts to solve more complex challenges.

P. 248

Designers United

Based in Thessaloniki, Greece, the award winning multidisciplinary design firm creates integrated design solutions for international clients from diverse industries. The studio's focuses encompass creative direction, branding, book and magazine design, web design and development, illustration, collateral and social-media/public-relations.

P. 128-131

Dijk, Sander van

Dijk believes that he can make a difference in the world to let people gain a different perspective on things. For that to happen Dijk translates great ideas into a high-end animation experience. Contributing animations driven by a great idea makes him more passionate about his biggest passion. The never ending and ever extending world of animation is what he called home.

P. 245

Emily Forgot

Emily Forgot is the moniker of London-based designer and illustrator Emily Alston who graduated from Liverpool School of Art and Design in 2004. Approaching all briefs with creative thoughts, humour and beauty in mind, Emily Forgot develops her own range of products for 'forgot shop' and commercial projects for clients big and small.

P. 103-104

Engesvik, Andreas

Creating furniture, tableware and products for international clients such as Iittala, Muuto, Ligne Roset and Asplund, Engesvik founded his own studio in 2009 and won numerous awards. He is currently also a guest professor at The University College of Arts, Crafts and Design (Konstfack) in Stockholm.

P. 027

Estrada, Jorge R. Canedo

Born in 1990 and raised in Bolivia, the designer is a strong believer in audio-driven animation. He loves typography; and he will spend hours walking outside in the rain or creating the perfect curve of animation.

P. 246

Fabio Ongarato Design

Founded in 1992 by partners Fabio Ongarato and Ronnen Goren, the studio is renowned for the diversity of its work with an open approach to graphic design varying from print and exhibitions to advertising with hints of passion for architecture, photography and contemporary art. Based in Melbourne, they work across fashion, corporate, arts and architecture and everything in between.

P. 088-089

Face.

Founded in 2006, Face is an intelligence-driven supermodernist design studio with a global perspective. Based in Monterrey, Mexico, Face.'s work range includes advertising, editorial projects, custom publishing, corporate identity and brand development.

P. 011, 058

Featherstone, Jack

A graphic artist based in London whose spans design, illustration, moving image and three-dimensional work.

P. 068-069

Fernández, Clara

Fernández is a young graphic designer at a marketing agency and student at Buenos Aires University. She also freelances and develops personal projects. She relishes working on disciplines such as illustration and typography based on her passion for purity, simplicity and clean structures.

P. 184-185

Fons Hickmann m23

Founded in 2001 by Gesine Grotrian-Steinweg and Fons Hickmann, the Berlin-based studio is one of today's most awarded design studios worldwide. The studio focuses on communication systems from print to cross-media design.

P. 182-183

Fredrika, Maija

A fine artist from Turku, Finland, Fredrika who works mostly on three-dimensional objects and illustrations.

P. 050-051

FriendsWithYou

Established by Miami-based artists Samuel Borkson and Arturo Sandoval III in 2002, the art collaborative spreads magic, luck, and friendship through large-scale experiential installations, public playgrounds, consumer products, as well as animation and multimedia projects. Their reductive and simplified use of geometric abstraction always contains a special injection of amusement and simple happiness found in everyday life.

P. 236-239

Gíslason, Thorleifur Gunnar

Having recently graduated from the Icelandic Academy of the Arts, Gíslason is now a graphic designer at Jónsson & Le'macks advertising agency, Reykjavík, and member of the multidisciplinary design crew, Wolfgang.

P. 036-037

Goolsby, Clark

Currently a painter and sculptor based in New York City, Goolsby graduated from the University of California at San Diego with a degree in Fine Arts in 2002. Goolsby's work explores diverse subjects with cryptic symbols, bold colours, patterns, and shapes.

P. 144-145

Grafica

An independent design and communication consultancy founded in Barcelona in 1993. They are specialised in print and digital materials, identity programmes, enviroments and products. The team works occasionally with Studio Astrid Stavro.

P. 228-231

Gray, Christopher

A designer and photographer living in London. Gray's work comprise of minimal compositions. He co-directs a gallery and studio space with Chris Read and splits his time curating events with living remotely in the Swedish countryside.

P. 142-143

Gunter, Ross

Currently working as a designer for Popcorn in east London, Gunter is a graphic designer specialising in multidisciplinary solutions for brand, print and screen, collaborating and producing work across all platforms with a focus on type.

P. 018, 044, 109

Hallée, Renaud

The founder of Possible Metrics, Hallée is a Montreal-based filmmaker creating music using visual systems. His musical short films has been shown in numerous music and film festivals around the globe, notably at SXSW, TIFF and Annecy.

P. 246

Happycentro

Founded in 1998 in Verona, Happycentro has worked for both big and small clients since then. Mixing complexity, order and fatigue is their formula for beauty. In addition to the commissioned work, the team always spends plenty of energy in research and testing on visual art, typography, graphic design, illustration, animation, film direction and music.

P. 136-137

Heath Killen Studio

Killen is a designer, strategist and design consultant from Newcastle, Australia. His work includes graphic design, interaction design and content development with frequent experimentation of new techniques and fields. His graphic design work always involves mixed media, with strong emphases on reducing elements down to their most essential and expressive forms.

P. 153, 166-171

Hey

A multidisciplinary design studio based in Barcelona, Spain specialising in brand management and editorial design, packaging and interactive design, Hey shares the profound conviction that good design means combining content, functionality, graphical expression and strategy.

P. 010, 040-041

Heydays

Based in Oslo, Heydays specialises in printed media, creative direction and graphic design on projects varying from corporate identity, interactive websites, magazines, books and packaging. Heydays strives to find balance between idea, function and aesthetics in every one of them.

P. 052-053

Hiromura Design Office

Born in Aichi prefecture in 1954 and joined Tanaka Ikko Design in 1977, the artist established his own design office in 1988. Hiromura has won numerous awards including the Mainichi Design Awards 2008, KU/KAN Award, 44th SDA Awards(Grand Prize) and Good Design Award (Gold Prize).

P. 196-201

Holderness, Carl

Working on various design disciplines, the born and bred Leeds-based designer specialises in identity design and typography-based solutions driven by layout and aesthetics for quality print and web distribution in the commercial and creative industries.

P. 074-075

Holy Grey

A collective founded in 2009 by Mariëlle van Genderen, Rob van Leijsen and Hanneke Minten. The like-minded graphic designers aim at critical self-initiated design projects.

P. 188-189

Hort

Founded by Eike Koenig, Hort began its inhabitance back in 1994 under former stage name 'EIKES GRAFISCHER HORT.' Hort is a creative playground where 'work' and 'play' can be said in the same sentence. Once a household name in the music industry, Hort is now a multidisciplinary creative hub known to draw ideas from things other than design.

P. 220-221

ICE CREAM FOR FREE™

The Berlin-based multidisciplinary design studio founded by Oliver Wiegner in 2005 is specialised on print. Current street and fine art scene in Berlin are the main inspiration for the studio's unique style.

P. 146-151

Iles, Mikell Fine

While growing up in the culturally diverse Mission district in San Francisco, the Brooklyn-based designer went to Clark Atlanta University to study graphic design and became fascinated with the music, murals, and graffiti that engulfed the world surrounding him. Iles has been working professionally since 2002. He's currently the Director of Design at digital agency, Noise.

P. 118-119

Joiner, Joe

An independent design creative who w across a variety of clientele, media and proach while also keen to produce indiv ally tailored, concept-led realisations.

P. 133

Kasper, Larissa & Florio, Rosari

Working mostly on printed matters wit strong focus on typography for the mus and cultural field, the two graphic design also run a studio collective together wi couple of friends in St.Gallen, Switzerlan

P. 025

Kelava, Josip

Graduated at Swinburne Faculty of Des the Croatian-born designer focuses graphic design, typography and photog phy. He is currently working for Clemer BBDO as a full-time senior designer.

P. 162-163

Keller Maurer Design

A graphic design consultancy based in nich. Formed in 2002 by Martina Keller Marcus Maurer, the collective's approac communication is one of simplicity and c ity, with content-driven and original des strategies in multiple disciplines and med

P. 084-085

Kelly, Johnny

Represented by Nexus Productions, Kell a London-based director and animator f Dublin before graduating from The Royal lege of Art with an MA in Animation and awarded the Conran Foundation Award the Provost, Sir Terence Conran. His grad tion short film, Procrastination, has been received and won him the Jerwood Mov Image Prize 08. The movie is now part of Saatchi & Saatchi New Director Showcas

P. 247

Khandelwal, Siddharth

Based in Mumbai. Khandelwal studied at University of Technology, Sydney and ch acterises his work with his endless pass and energy based on his guiding princi 'everything should be made as simple possible, not simpler. Siddharth began career with the strategy guru, Martin Li storm in Australia.

P. 124-125

Kim, Derek

A freelance designer specialising in iden typography, and poster design for cult establishments and small startup com nies. Kim also initiates personal projects t allow his creativity to expand into differ sectors besides design.

P. 116-117

Kleiner, Carl

Best known for his involvement in the making of IKEA's baking book "Homemade is best", the photographer and creative visualiser's portfolio reveals an intriguing understanding of composition and how objects gives and adds value to each other. Carl approaches each project with curiosity and openness, making for surprises in his images.

P. 138-141

Klipfel, Charles & Carnicelli, Quentin

The French duo has collaborated on a few films together under the name, "Tout court". Not limited by the technics, they love to play with basics shapes and colours.

P. 244

Lei Lei

A young Chinese multimedia animationist with hands-on skills in graphic design, illustration, cartoon, graffiti and music, Lei Lei founded animation group, Raydesign studio, in 2005 and obtained his master's degree in animation from Tsinghua University in 2009. His film, This is LOVE (2010) was screened at Ottawa International Animation Festival and awarded The Best Narrative Short.

P. 243, 245

Lesley Moore

The brainchild of Dutch designer Karin van den Brandt (b. 1975) and Norwegian-born Alex Clay (b.1974). Since Arnhem Academy of the Arts (now ArtEZ) their careers have intertwined. The two merged again after graduation whilst working as designers at Dutch agency De Designpolitie.

P. 190-193

Lo Siento

Creative agency set up by Borja Martinez in 2004 in Barcelona working mostly on craft materials and three-dimensional solutions, in a wide range of projects from packaging, music covers, editorial and graphic identities for restaurants and film production houses.

P. 014-015

Loop-Loop Studio

Founded by Boris Rodríguez, also designer at Manuel Estrada Design Studio and co-founder of Bürøgrafica, the Madrid-based design and illustration studio cares about concept and coherence of the discourse. To them, design is about creating fascinating stories.

P. 016-017

Machado, João Ricardo

Born in 1985, Machado is a Brazilian graphic designer and illustrator living and working in Portugal. Graduated in Design from University of South of Santa Catarina, Brazil, and with a degree on ESAD.CR, in Portugal, Machado always attempts to find a positive way in everything and enjoy bringing happiness to people, whoever they are.

P. 152

MAGA Atelier

José Mendes, Luís Alvoeiro and Carlos Guerreiro were long time colleagues before they formed MAGA in 2009. Driven by their love for design, MAGA develops tailored solutions in Lisbon (Chiado) according to individual needs and ambitions. They deem themselves a partner in the projects it takes.

P. 132, 134-135

Magpie Studio

Magpie provides strategic thought and clear market insight for national and international clients with solutions that are not only engaging but also clear in its message. The studio's solutions are based on listening and thorough understanding.

P. 020-021

Mark Gowing Design

Mark Gowing has been a design professional since 1987. His work has been awarded, exhibited and published the world over. In 2008 Mark became the first Australian to win the Gold Medal at the International Poster Biennale in Warsaw. Mark is the director of Mark Gowing Design and curator of the AGDA Poster Annual.

P. 032

Markevičius, Tomas

The motion/print designer based in Vilnius, Lithuania, is currently working at TAPE, a video and design studio and freelancing. He is obsessed with various geometric shapes whether they are still or in motion.

P. 247

Marnich Associates

Based in Barcelona, Marnich is a design and communication consultancy believing in simplicity and clarity. Their clients range from small restaurants, independent publishers and music festival to large corporations, banks and museums.

P. 012

Matic, Viktor

Born in 1987 in former Yugoslavia near Sarajevo, Matic grew up in Croatia, Germany and Italy, and pursued studies in product design and visual communication in Italy, Israel and Turkey. Matic is a designer, ideas creator, label founder and event manager on a range of cultural and commercial projects, based in South Tyrol, Italy

P. 028

McLean, Chantelle Kamala

A freelance graphic designer currently living in London. After graduating in fashion design at Central Saint Martins she realised her creative eye focused on strong image, colour and print. She graduated from a Design for Visual Communication postgraduate course at London College of Communication.

P. 154-155

Milkxhake

An independent graphic design studio in Hong Kong founded by Chinese graphic designer Javin Mo in 2006, Milkxhake advocates the power of visual communication to visual branding, identity, print and website. By bringing up creative ideas and unique visual languages, Milkxhake is highly acclaimed for quality with unique design approach, recognised by numerous international design awards.

P. 204-207

Mind Design

Based in London, the independent graphic design studio is founded by Holger Jacobs after his graduation from the Royal College of Art in 1999. Mind design specialises in visual identities and has worked for a wide range of clients in different sectors.

P. 022-023

Mister

With 15 years of experience in blending design, technology and branding, Mister creates modern interactive experiences and designs for screen, mobiles and print. Mister works in partnership with ambitious clients and create compelling design to ensure great impact in their brand.

P. 098-099

Motherbird

Motherbird is a Melbourne-based creative outfit consisting of Jack Mussett, Chris Murphy and Dan Evans. The trio have collaborated for big clients including MTV, Qantas, Warner Music and Positive Posters. Motherbird specialises in brand identity, print design, image making, packaging and environmental signage. In 2010 they were awarded the nation-wide 'Spirit of Youth Award' (SOYA) as well as being on the Australian Graphic Design Association (AGDA) council.

P. 104-105, 158-159

mousegraphics

mousegraphics is a creative office that has been realising this basic principle since 1984. Their approach has been rewarded with a significant circle of longstanding cooperations and new and successful professional relationships in wide-ranging applications within the design field. mousegraphics is a member of EDEE, the Greek association of advertising and communication agencies and also member of Design lobby."

P. 059

Mr Kaplin

Mr Kaplin is the creative partnership of Robert Glassford and Daniel Zucco, who joined forces in 2011. Primarily focusing on directing, animation and motion design, Mr Kaplin has built a network of clients in Japan and Australia including artists like Toob, Frank Eddie, Chinza Dopeness and Paris Wells. Last year their music video for Paris Wells won the Melbourne Design Awards for Best Motion. The directing duo have just relocated to London.

P. 247

Mucho

Mucho is a graphics design studio focusing on visual communication. Their service includes art direction, corporate identity, editorial design, packaging, graphic communications, digital design and motion graphics.

P. 046-047

MusaWorkLab™

A design and communication studio founded in 2003 by Raquel Viana, Paulo Lima and Ricardo Alexandre, based in Lisbon, Portugal. Musa develops projects mainly in the areas of fashion and culture while also carrying several activities and events to promote the Portuguese design internationally.

P. 026

MUSCLEBEAVER

A design collective from Munich, founded by Andreas Kronbeck and Tobias Knipf, who have worked as a team since 2005 in animation, illustration and graphic design.

P. 244

MWM Graphics

Founded by Matt W. Moore and led by David Ruiz, MWM Graphics is a Portland-based design and illustration studio specialising in innovative brand concepts and codes, corporate identity, advertising, packaging and broadcast design, honoured with more than 100 national and international awards. Matt works across disciplines, from colourful digital illustrations in his signature "Vectorfunk" style to freeform watercolour paintings and massive aerosol murals. Matt is also the founder of Core Deco and co-founder and designer for Glyph Cue Clothing.

P. 232-235

Neubau (NeubauBerlin.Com)

Austrian-born designer Stefan Gandl formed Neubau in Berlin in 2001 before taking the world by storm with the release of their two bestsellers, Neubau Welt (2005) and Neubau Modul (2007). In 2008 Neubau exhibited "Neubauism", a perspicacious, kinetic journey through the world of Neubau, opened by legendary designer Wim Crouwel in the Netherlands. Neubau operates through commissions, developing design and typography for print, screen and space.

P. 056-057

Nick Bell Design

Specialising in designing three-dimensional interactive environments, Nick Bell Designer collaborates with architects, museum directors and curators on exhibitions interpretation design, digital interactive design, audio/visual media design and wayfinding. Their work for the Science Museum, Imperial War Museum, The Wellcome Trust, V&A, Tate, Tyne & Wear Museums and the British Council has helped these institutions winning many industry awards, including The Council of Europe Museum Prize, an Interpret Britain and Ireland Award and a DBA Design Effectiveness Gold Award.

P. 090-091

Non-Format

Established in London in 2000 by Kjell Ekhorn and Jon Forss, the two-man team works on a diverse range of projects including art direction, design, illustration and custom typography for numeral international brands. After Forss relocated to Minneapolis and Ekhorn returned to his native Norway in 2009, Skype™ becomes the bridge for their partnership on every project.

P. 062-063

Officemilano

Specialising in brand identity and art direction, Matteo Carrubba and Angela Tomasoni founded Officemilano in Milan. Their ability to design all the aspects of branding, from naming to the development on print, advertising, web and multimedia channels is the key feature and DNA of Officemilano.

P. 060-061

Oh Yeah Studio

Founding Oh Yeah Studio in 2008, Hans Christian Øren and Christina Magnussen met in Central Saint Martins London when they both studied graphic and communication design and illustration and has been working together ever since. The duo shares the same desire and belief that design is a way of living and it should be fun. This is also the vision behind Oh Yeah studio.

P. 160-161

Ohashi, Takashi

Ohashi is a motion image artist and "Motion Designer" based in Tokyo. He creates animation works and motion image installations that examine the relation between vision and music. His speciality is in animation that synchronizes visuals and music. He has recently participated in music video for HIFANA.

P. 244

ONIONSKIN

An animation collective set up by Toshikazu Tamura and Ai Sugaya from the Tokyo University of the Arts who have been working together since 2011.

P. 242

Ozay, Savas

Savas Ozay is a Istanbul-based independent art director and designer. Since 2000, he has experimented and mastered many aspects of design including typography, web, art direction, mobile platforms, interaction, illustration, motion and branding.

P. 248

Parallax Design

As one of Australia's most creative studios, the brand and communications design consultancy is reputed on strategic thinking and being able to distill complex problems into simple, logical solutions through thorough understanding of clients' objectives.

P. 076-077, 123

Patternity

A creative consultancy driven by the certainty that pattern is everywhere, from mundane to magnificent, the heart of their projects lays the belief that pattern positively engages them with the environment.

P. 172-173

Qu, Kelvin

Born in 1979, Qu studied in HKU SPACE in 2012. He is member of New York ADC, ICOGRADA, CDA, CCII, as well as founder and creative director of Roncham Design Office, specialising in brand consulting and design.

P. 202-203

Raw Color

Raw Color is a collaboration of the Designers Christoph Brach and Daniera ter Haar. In their Eindhoven-based studio, the duo displays a desire to conduct a primary research and question meanings driven by curiosity. Their work reflect a sophisticated treatment of material by mixing the fields of photography and graphic design.

P. 156-157

Re-public

Re-public is a graphic design agency, specialising in visual identity and communication design. We engage ourselves with ideas, products, brand values and communication challenges and translate them into competent and inspiring design solutions. Our work gives new life to brands and help people communicate effectively.

P. 042-043

Resort Studio

Founded in 2012 by Michael Häne and Dieter Glauser, both studied at the Zürich University of the Arts, Resort conceives and design identities, digital media and printed matter for companies, institutions and individual with a cultural or economic background.

P. 024

Rodchester, Amy

A young graphic designer and illustrator based in Leeds, England who enjoys pushing the boundaries and challenging her typographic and illustrative skills, especially in 3D forms. Photography is a big part of her creative thinking in terms of capturing moments and experiences that inspire me.

P. 186-187

Ruffeo Hearts Lil Snotty

Designers R. Mackswell Sherman and Sara Jones gaze towards the future for their inspiration, creating a look that is timeless and unique. The streetwear brand is known for its aesthetics and ethics. All designs are made in NYC.

P. 174-175